improvers

IT'S YOUR MOVE

CHRIS WARD

D0912704

EVERYMAN CHESS

Everyman Publishers plc   www.everyman.uk.com

First published in 2001 by Everyman Publishers plc, formerly Cadogan Books plc, Gloucester Mansions, 140A Shaftesbury Avenue, London WC2H 8HD

British Library Cataloguing-in-Publication Data
A catalogue record for this book is available from the British Library.

ISBN 1 85744 278 4

Distributed in North America by The Globe Pequot Press, P.O Box 480, 246 Goose Lane, Guilford, CT 06437-0480.

All other sales enquiries should be directed to Everyman Chess, Gloucester Mansions, 140A Shaftesbury Avenue, London WC2H 8HD
tel: 020 7539 7600 fax: 020 7379 4060
email: dan@everyman.uk.com
website: www.everyman.uk.com

EVERYMAN CHESS SERIES (formerly Cadogan Chess)
Chief Advisor: Garry Kasparov
Commissioning editor: Byron Jacobs

Typeset and edited by First Rank Publishing, Brighton.
Production by Book Production Services.
Printed and bound in Great Britain by The Cromwell Press Ltd., Trowbridge, Wiltshire.

Contents

Introduction   5

Test One   7

Test Two   27

Test Three   47

Test Four   67

Test Five   87

Test One - Solutions   107

Test Two - Solutions   115

Test Three - Solutions   122

Test Four - Solutions   129

Test Five - Solutions   136

Marking Scheme and Scorechart   144

Introduction

Hello and welcome to *It's Your Move 2*. This time it's personal! Well, that and the fact that this sequel is aimed at improvers! Yes, perhaps I was a little mean in my first volume. Hence this time the questions are a touch easier although, I hasten to add, no less informative. Indeed, rather than extracting the test positions from real life games, this time I have compiled the teasers myself to get your brains ticking over. If this book works as planned then you will be introduced to some useful opening principles, some interesting middlegame plans and some critical endgame theory; all in a fun way.

Of course if it doesn't, then I've failed. Sorry about that!

Meet the Panel

Taking you through this book are another set of lovable characters:

'Anxious' Amy
All of her friends say that Amy is a bit of a worrier! She's not a great fan of uncertainty and likes to get things sorted out quickly. Amy is a fairly solid chess player whose main weak point is that she doesn't like taking risks. A very nervous individual, she likes to play things by the book and is often flustered when hit by a surprise.

'Barmy' Bill
Bill isn't always 'with it'. People say that he is as unpredictable in life as he is with the chess pieces. He might be a genius one moment and a complete fruitcake the next! You will indeed observe throughout this book that he will provide some fantastic ideas. Unfortunately the majority of his conclusions are garbage so you'd better be very confident when backing him!

'Cheeky' Chuck
Chuck enjoys life to the full and loves his chess. Always playing

pranks on his mates, he relishes coming up with sneaky plans to defeat the other members of his local chess club. Be careful though when deciding to follow his advice as he does try to pull the odd fast one. What may appear to Chuck to be a candidate for 'subtlety of the year' award may in fact be the duffest sequence of moves ever seen!

'Dithering' Debbie

Debbie has lots of good ideas. In fact it's fair to say too many as her main problem in life is deciding between one thing or another. Instead of getting several good things done, nothing happens at all. Consequently she's not always very convincing in her arguments but I can guarantee you that there is quality material in there!

'Electric' Eric

Some still believe Eric received the nickname 'Electric' following an unfortunate experience with a screwdriver and a temperamental toaster. Judging by the way that his hair sticks up, one would indeed tend to think that this is the case. However the truth though is that his opponents have sarcastically (and rather cruelly) labelled him 'Electric' as reference to his rather uninteresting style of play. Not the most exciting of individuals, his style is a little tedious. Nevertheless though he rarely goes out on a limb, one can't deny that he often gets results and there is no mistaking that tiny smile that appears when his bored opponents finally throw in the towel.

With each question it is our panel of 'experts' who must provide answers. It is your task to ascertain which of them offers the most accurate solution. Note that there is never more than one completely correct answer (and a maximum score of 10 points per question – 100 points per test), although I do often award points for good tries. You'll soon get the hang of it and, most important of all, hopefully learn something.

Well that's it from me. I would say 'good luck' but I'd rather not encourage pure guessing! If it's okay by you then, I'll simply say 'goodbye' and hope you enjoy the book.

Chris Ward
London, October 2001

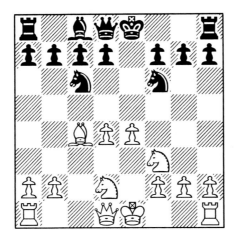

Black to play
White has managed to obtain two nice looking pawns in the centre.
Should Black, to move, take immediate steps to address this situa-
tion?

Amy
Amy wants to play 1...d6 because she is very worried about the possibility of White further advancing his e-pawn. She doesn't really
want to get pushed back and has it in mind to attack e4 a little
later.

Bill
Bill likes 1...h5 because this adds protection to his king's knight
when it ultimately moves to g4. Assuming White is likely to castle
kingside, if he should play h3 Black could then even leave the knight
attacked with the intention of recapturing with his h-pawn and
opening the file.

Chuck

Chuck favours 1...h6 because he feels that it is so often a useful move in symmetrical e-pawn openings such as this. After he castles he will never have to worry about back rank mates and he has even created a retreat square, if required, for his f6-knight.

Debbie

Debbie feels the need to take immediate action against White's pawn centre. She has eventually elected to attempt to break up White's powerful duo with 1...d5, although she thought long and hard about a temporary piece sacrifice. Indeed Debbie was left undecided about 1...♘xe4, intending to regain the piece with a pawn fork in the event of 2 ♘xe4.

Eric

It's the solid 1...0-0 for Eric, who is a strong believer in castling early. The king is put into safety and he can swiftly bring his rook into action on the e-file.

| ☐ Amy | ☐ Bill | ☐ Chuck | ☐ Debbie | ☐ Eric |

Points: ....10......

White to play
In this rook and pawn versus rook endgame the black rook finds itself passively defending against White's back rank threats. Can you suggest a winning plan for the first player?

Amy
Amy wants to play 1 f7. She believes that this f-pawn is the key to her converting this position and, after the black rook vacates the e-file, she can put her own rook on e6 and then down to e8. Black has nothing constructive to do in the meantime.

Bill
Bill has a similar idea to Amy but ultimately wants to check on g8 rather than e8. He also believes that 1 f7 is tactically flawed and can wait before playing it. His several stage plan is to 'pass' now with the rook, play f6-f7 and then put his king on f6. After this he will manoeuvre his rook to the g-file and ♖g8+ should be game, set and match!

Chuck

Chuck doesn't like the idea of advancing his f-pawn at all at the moment. In fact he believes that a simple winning plan involves manoeuvring his rook so that it will be able to give a check on h8. He understands that the black rook can't leave the back rank because then a check would lead to a winning king and pawn endgame, so he has in mind 1 ♖a7-h7 and, given the opportunity, ♖h8 mate. Only if Black then moves his king will White be tempted by f6-f7(+).

Debbie

Debbie feels that she could suggest many winning plans but she is not going to bother. They are merely attempts but, since 'All rook endings are drawn', nothing is likely to be successful.

Eric

Eric thinks that if Black plays sensibly, White will not be able to win while the rooks remain. Therefore his simple idea is to reposition his king on d7. This will be a little tricky but it is definitely possible, after which he can force a trade of rooks by moving his own to c8.

☐ Amy   ☐ Bill   ☐ Chuck   ☐ Debbie   ☐ Eric

Points: ....

10

White to play

In this practical king and pawn endgame, what is White's best move and how should he continue after that?

Amy

Amy doesn't like her king lagging behind and believes 1 ♔e3 to be correct (and worth the c5-pawn). Expecting that the black king will later be distracted by her passed g-pawn, she anticipates being able to net all three black pawns in quick succession.

Bill

Bill wants to go it alone with his c-pawn. After 1 c6 ♔e6 (the only way to stop this pawn) 2 c7 ♔d7 he acknowledges that his c-pawn is doomed but believes that to be of little consequence as his g-pawn will promote.

Chuck

Chuck isn't convinced that Bill has calculated correctly. He likes 1 c6 but after 1...♔e6 prefers the idea of 2 g4. His logic is that the black king will be stretched through trying to stop both white pawns from promoting. Chuck is mildly concerned about leaving Black with two connected passed pawns but considers that they will not be a major problem on their own.

Debbie

Debbie isn't sure about either 1 c6 or 1 cxd6 and, having heard much stuff about the something known as the 'opposition', she can't be sure as to which is the most accurate square on which to put her king. What she does know, though, is that 'passed pawns are meant to be pushed' so she feels that she cannot go wrong with 1 g4.

Eric

Eric believes that he has found a risk-free route to victory. After 1 cxd6 ♔xd6 2 ♔e3, whether Black opts to defend his e-pawn with his king on e5 or d5, White will use his g-pawn as a deflector. After the inevitable trade of g- for e-pawn, his king will be in the dominant position of being able to snap up Black's a-pawn. With the black king so offside it will be game over!

☐ Amy	☐ Bill	☐ Chuck	☐ Debbie	☐ Eric

Points: ....

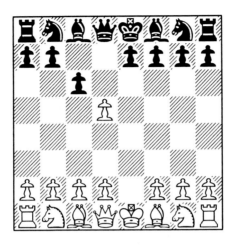

White to play

Rather than simply recapturing the pawn on d5 with the queen or, indeed, attacking it with ...♘f6, Black has unleashed the surprise move ...c6. What is White's best response?

Amy

Amy believes that she has seen this sacrifice before. Instead of grabbing a 'hot' pawn she is anxious to get some pieces developed. Her proposal of 1 ♗c4 protects the pawn where it stands on d5 and looks through to the typical weak point 'f7'.

Bill

Bill can't believe Black's nerve! Yes – 'a pawn is a pawn' is his view and he will begin his development after the obvious 1 dxc6.

Chuck

Chuck has heard that it is often good to refuse gambits such as this. He has never seen this before but recommends 1 d6. White will not emerge a pawn up but nor will he promote quick development for Black.

Debbie

Initially unsure of which knight to develop, Debbie now favours 1 ♘c3 because it retains the focus on the vital d5-square.

Eric

'Put your pawns in the centre' is the motto that Eric likes to adhere to, and he believes that White should ignore the confusion regarding d5 and c6. His opinion is that 1 d4 can't be a bad move and should therefore be played now.

☐ Amy ☐ Bill ☐ Chuck ☐ Debbie ☐ Eric

Points: ....

Black to play

It is Black to play and there will be an added white piece on d3 (a pawn, knight or bishop). Given the options below (as White), what would you rather have, and why?

Amy

Amy wants a pawn. Her reasoning is that while pieces are very good in the opening and middlegame, in the endgame one wants to be thinking about promoting pawns.

Bill

Bill has a fondness for the unpredictability of knights. Unlike bishops they can capture enemy pawns on both light and dark squares, and he predicts a quick fork will occur to begin the notching up of pawns.

Chuck

Chuck would also prefer to have a knight. His winning plan would then be to post his knight on the queenside and, while this sector is under surveillance, the king can clear out the kingside. Then the monarch can return to where the real action is and do the same there, too.

Debbie

Debbie understands that the long-range ability of the bishop is better in endgames with pawns on both flanks. However, she is not sure if this is applicable here because White has no pawns on the kingside. Nonetheless her idea is to bring her king over to the queenside as soon as possible while her bishop monitors the passed black h-pawns.

Eric

With a bishop on d3 Eric believes converting this endgame would be a piece of cake. His view is that pawns and bishops combine well together because, if necessary, they can look after each other. Although a bishop is unable to alter the colour complex upon which it operates it can always control useful squares. The king is around to capture any pawns and he suggests that the white monarch should first set its sights on the h-pawns. With these captured the king can then return to the queenside to ultimately secure victory.

☐ Amy ☐ Bill ☐ Chuck ☐ Debbie ☐ Eric

Points: ....

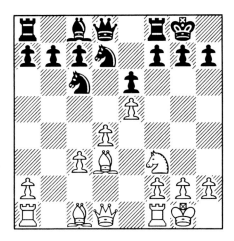

White to play

White clearly has a comfortable space advantage thanks to the impressive central pawn chain. Can you suggest a plan for him to make progress?

Amy

Amy is a bit worried about the potential of Black's knights. She suggests 1 ♗b5, when one of them will be captured, possibly with the additional bonus of doubling Black's pawns.

Bill

There is no beating about the bush for Bill, who is all for the sacrifice 1 ♗xh7+, justifying his decision after analysing 1...♔xh7 2 ♘g5+. The white queen will come into play and Black will be mated, or will at least lose material.

Chuck

Chuck wants to threaten mate in a more restrained manner. His e5-

pawn offers good cover for the e4-square and so he likes 1 ♕e2, with the simple idea of 2 ♕e4. If Black ultimately defends with ...g7-g6 then the dark squares will have been irrevocably weakened, while ...f7-f5 will result in an isolated e-pawn after an en passant capture.

Debbie
Debbie can't quite decide which rook to move. 1 ♖e1 doesn't look bad but as it brings the rook to a half-open file she favours 1 ♖b1.

Eric
The only minor piece not yet moved is the dark-squared bishop and it is therefore of no great surprise that Eric recommends completing his development in that department with 1 ♗g5. Black must then deal with the attack on his queen and White can work on allocating new homes for his own queen and rooks.

☐ Amy	☐ Bill	☐ Chuck	☐ Debbie	☐ Eric

Points: ....

White to play

White's king is obviously going to be instrumental in his winning this endgame but until it appears on the scene he must take care not to lose his remaining pawn. How should White go about safeguarding it?

Amy

Amy has observed that 1...♚b6 is a serious threat and proposes the immediate 1 a7. Then, after 1...♚b7, the required protection can be provided with 2 ♘b5. As both the knight and pawn are then effectively immune from capture, White will have all the time in the world (or 50 moves, whichever comes first!) to bring her king over and secure victory.

Bill

Amy has informed Bill that she could equally play 1 ♘b5+ ♚b6 2 a7 ♚b7 etc. but Bill's suggestion requires accuracy. After 1 a7 ♚b7 he is sure that 2 ♘c6 is the only way to ensure things work out.

Chuck

Chuck has a crazy idea of 1 ♘c6 with the intention of meeting 1...♚b6 with 2 ♘b8. If the knight is ever taken, the pawn will promote.

Debbie

Uncertain of how to arrange things on the queenside, Debbie wants to bring back her king immediately (starting with 1 ♚g2). Moreover, king centralisation in endgames is always recommended in textbooks.

Eric

Eric feels that supporting the pawn where it stands will offer White more room for manoeuvre. Consequently he would like to play either 1 ♘e6+ or 1 ♘b3, both with the intention of 2 ♘c5.

☐ Amy　　☐ Bill　　☐ Chuck　　☐ Debbie　☐ Eric

Points: ....

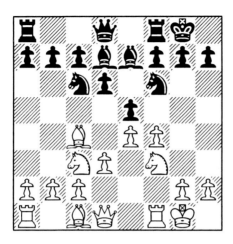

White to play

White has done well to comfortably arrange the 'pawn break' f2-f4, whilst Black has developed rather passively. Can you suggest a way for White to progress?

Amy

Amy is eager to open things up in the centre. The sequence she proposes is 1 fxe5 dxe5 2 d4, which will maximise the activity of the bishops.

Bill

Although it might appear somewhat bizarre Bill wants to relocate his bishop on b5 instead. Theoretically this is his bad bishop, and trading it for its opposite number on d7 will improve his position.

Chuck

Chuck feels that White has an edge on the queenside and now is the time to get to grips with the queenside, too. An expansion policy with 1 a3 and 2 b4 is what he has in mind.

Debbie

Debbie wants to go with her kingside initiative. After 1 f5 she believes that expansion on the kingside is the best policy. She is not entirely sure of the form this should take but somehow arranging g4-g5 would be nice.

Eric

Knights love outposts and, although d5 is not one exactly, there is little doubt that it is an attractive location for a white steed. Indeed, after 1 ♘d5 Bill's argument is that Black cannot capture as 1...♘xd5 2 exd5 will mean dropping the e5-pawn.

☑ Amy   ☐ Bill   ☐ Chuck   ☐ Debbie   ☐ Eric

Points: ....

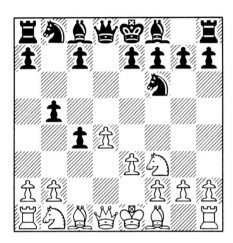

White to play
White has had his 'Queen's Gambit' accepted and now Black has set his stall out to look after the pawn on c4. How should White deal with Black's stubbornness?

Amy
Amy believes that White should not waste time and thus suggests beginning the undermining of Black's b5-pawn immediately. For her the only move is 1 a4.

Bill
Bill thinks that because Black is (voluntarily) exposed along the b7-g2 diagonal the key move is 1 ♘e5. Exerting further pressure on c4, this would also introduce the possibility of ♕f3.

Chuck
Chuck likes 1 ♘a3. He acknowledges that, normally, 'knights on the rim are dim' but the text would pressurise the two vital elements in

Black's position, namely the pawns on b5 and c4.

Debbie
Debbie thinks that Amy has a point but, true to the concept of a gambit, she prefers 1 b3. Black will be a pawn up after 1...cxb3 2 ♕xb3 but the b5-pawn then comes under pressure and White will enjoy both superior development and central control.

Eric
According to Eric the gambit has served its purpose of providing White with an extra pawn in the centre. He believes there is no future for his bishop on the f1-c4 diagonal and naturally sees 1 g3 and 2 ♗g2 is the most obvious way for him to castle.

☐ Amy	☐ Bill	☐ Chuck	☐ Debbie	☐ Eric

Points: ....

White to play

White has a comfortable material advantage in this endgame but must be careful to guard against complacency. Whose selected first move is the only one that would NOT be successful if best play (for both sides) then followed?

Amy

Amy wants to retrieve her king as quickly as possible. There is no time like the present, and she votes for 1 ♔g7.

Bill

Bill proposed 1 ♗b7 but then looked a little sheepish and may well have wanted to reconsider.

Chuck

1 bxa7+ ♔xa7 2 ♗b7 is adequate according to Chuck, who will later use his king to help flush Black's monarch out of the corner.

Debbie

Debbie has opted for Chuck's 1 bxa7+ but (after 1...♔xa7), caught between the bishop's two defending moves, selects 2 ♗f1.

Eric

There is no doubt for Eric that 1 b7 is the simplest continuation. With the pawn supported on b7 his king can return to action at leisure.

☐ Amy	☐ Bill	☐ Chuck	☐ Debbie	☐ Eric
Points:				

White to play
It is White to play in this king and pawn ending. Who is better and why?

Amy
Amy feels that Black is better because, after 1 a5 ♔c5, Black's king will be able to take White's a-pawn, and then b-pawn, well before White can capture the h-pawns and return.

Bill
Bill also prefers Black because his king occupies the more dominant post and he has a useful 3 to 2 pawn majority.

Chuck
Chuck feels that White's supported passed a-pawn gives him the upper hand. As Black's king will never be able to approach and capture on b3, White can more or less do what he wants.

Debbie

Not the most committal of people, Debbie has implied that the position is level and almost certain (i.e. with reasonable play from both sides) to be a draw.

Eric

Eric has given a great deal of thought to the position and has decided that the correct sequence of moves will result in White promoting to a queen and Black having a pawn on the 7th rank. This will be a theoretical draw.

□ Amy   □ Bill   □ Chuck   □ Debbie   □ Eric

Points: ....

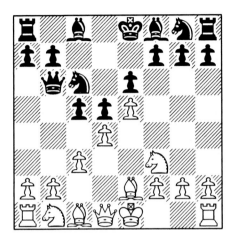

Black to play

White has a typical space advantage in this Advance variation of the French Defence. Black doesn't want to find himself being further squashed, so how might he react in order to generate some activity?

Amy

Amy believes that Black should create space of her own. For her the queenside is where the action is and, after 1...c4, Black has a long-term aim of expanding with ...b7-b5 and ...b5-b4.

Bill

Bill recommends serious action on the kingside in the form of 1...h6 and, if allowed, 2...g5. This will give Black some room in this sector and help to pressurise White's centre.

Chuck

Chuck feels that Black should allocate his resources to attacking

White's d4-pawn. Therefore he likes 1...♘ge7 (but would consider 1...♘h6) in order to develop this knight on f5.

Debbie
Debbie feels that the black f-pawn has a role to play and has opted for the central challenge 1...f6 rather than the more blocking 1...f5. Either move should improve Black's space situation.

Eric
Eric definitely wants to develop his g8-knight but doesn't like 1...♘h6, while he feels that on e7 the knight simply obstructs his bishop. However, he has come up with the solution: the sequence 1...cxd4 2 cxd4 ♝b4+ with ...♘ge7 to follow gives him just what he wants.

☐ Amy	☐ Bill	☐ Chuck	☐ Debbie	☐ Eric
Points:				

White to play
As White, *don't panic* just yet as you have a rook to be added.
Where would you prefer to put it and why?

Amy
Amy wants the rook on a3 so that it can immediately go to b3.
There it keeps an eye on the b2-pawn and pins the one on c3.

Bill
Bill would prefer it on c2 so that it can go to d2 to check the black
king, a clever rook sacrifice that leads to stalemate and secures
White the desired draw.

Chuck
For Chuck the solution is to have the rook on e1 so that it can go to
e3. Chuck likes this sneaky rook sacrifice that will enable his king to
blockade the pawns and hold the draw.

Debbie

Debbie likes a bit of flexibility. On h8 her rook would have options and she would use ♖d8+ to help her king reach the comforting c2-post.

Eric

Eric loves to blockade passed pawns with rooks because then they will go no further. He is a little worried about keeping it on b1, though, due to ...c3-c2+. However, from b1 it can nudge to c1, monitoring the pawns and making a drawn king and pawn versus king ending imminent.

☐ Amy	☐ Bill	☐ Chuck	☑ Debbie	☐ Eric

Points: ...10......

White to play
White is a supported passed pawn up in this ending, but is there a plan for him to win?

Amy
Amy believes White's best chance is with 1 a6, deflecting the black king in order to gain entry into White's queenside.

Bill
Bill believes that this position is simple. White should basically ignore what is happening elsewhere and send his king directly to f5.

Chuck
Chuck agrees with Bill but wants to monitor Black's pawns carefully. After 1 ♔e3 h5, for example, he wants to play 2 g4, whilst in reply to 1...g5 he intends 2 h4.

Debbie

Debbie had difficulty choosing between 1 h4 and 1 g4 but eventually opted for the latter. The idea is to help provide a route into the kingside for White's king.

Eric

For Eric 1 h4 is the only accurate move that provides White with the necessary squares for the key entry into Black's position.

☐ Amy   ☐ Bill   ☐ Chuck   ☐ Debbie   ☐ Eric

Points: ....

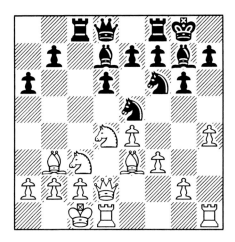

White to play
Black has quite a solid looking position. How might White try to break it down?

Amy
Black looks to have ...b5 in mind and so Amy suggests clamping down with 1 a4. A restriction policy should prove more than adequate to frustrate her opponent.

Bill
Bill feels that Black has irrevocably weakened the b6-square and that this should be punished. Beginning with 1 ♕f2 White can plan to plant a bishop there, whilst a knight invasion, too, would not be far behind.

Chuck
Blasting through the centre is White's solution. 1 ♖he1 is Chuck's preference, with his intention being the arrangement of f4 and e5.

After this the majority of Black's pieces will be embarrassed, with White's springing to life.

Debbie

Debbie feels that, as this is a position with opposite sides castling, a kingside attack is most appropriate. After first considering 1 ♗h6 she is instead leaning towards the pawn sacrifice 1 h5. The intention is to blast open the h-file for White's major pieces in order to ultimately deliver checkmate.

Eric

Eric wants to play it cool. He feels that White has no weaknesses and he certainly doesn't want to start creating any now. Quiet moves, beginning with 1 ♔b1, and moving on to the likes of g2-g3 and a2-a3, for example, will leave Black regretting his choice of opening.

☐ Amy   ☐ Bill   ☐ Chuck   ☐ Debbie   ☐ Eric

Points: ....

White to play
The white king appears to have its work cut out in this fascinating king and pawn ending. What exactly should it be doing?

Amy
Amy wants to go for the c-pawn with her king and then get back in time for the g-pawn. With these troublemakers removed she will easily promote one of her own pawns.

Bill
Bill is thinking like Amy but believes that it is vital that the king goes for the g-pawn first. Only then should White return for the c-pawn.

Chuck
Chuck has a sneaky sequence in mind. After 1 ♔d5 g4 2 a8♕+ ♔xa8 3 ♔c6 g3 4 ♔c7 g2 5 b7+ ♔a7 6 b8♕+ ♔a6 7 ♕b6 is mate. Beautiful!

Debbie

Debbie feels that chasing either black pawn prove to be futile because the other will simply push forward. She does not want to be pulled from pillar to post and so suggests holding ground in the middle with her king.

Eric

Eric thinks he has a clever idea, too. Forgetting about Black's passed pawns, he wants to advance his king up the board, only to sacrifice his a-pawn at the right time in order to aid the promotion of his b-pawn.

☐ Amy   ☐ Bill   ☐ Chuck   ☐ Debbie   ☐ Eric

Points: ....

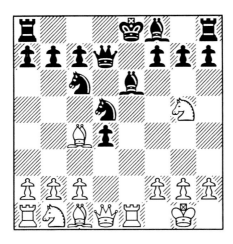

White to play
In this middlegame (the opening being the Italian Game) White is contemplating the outrageous 1 ♘xf7. How would you assess this sacrifice?

Amy
It's brilliant. Whichever way Black chooses to take the knight, he is destined to lose.

Bill
Bill loves sacrifices but believes this one fails since Black has a choice of three perfectly good recaptures.

Chuck
Amazingly Chuck thinks that it is Black who has all the fun. Upon 1 ♘xf7 Black should sacrifice the h8-rook by 1...0-0-0. The knight will be trapped in the corner and Black's excellent central control will provide him with excellent compensation for the exchange.

Debbie

Debbie feels that both 1...♕xf7 and 1...♔xf7 would highlight White's idea as dubious, but probably prefers the former.

Eric

According to Eric 1 ♘xf7 would be strong were it not for 1...♔xf7. Black then has everything covered and it wouldn't be worth a piece just to prevent Black from castling.

☐ Amy   ☐ Bill   ☐ Chuck   ☐ Debbie   ☐ Eric

Points: ....

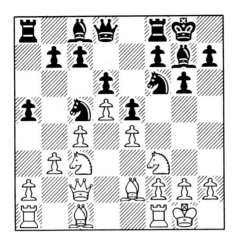

Black to play
Black, to play, is close to completing his development. Can you suggest a move now and a plan for the middlegame?

Amy
Amy is a bit worried about having such a poor bishop on g7. She suggests a plan to trade it off for White's (good) dark-squared bishop. Here 1...h5 heralds a simple plan of ...♔h7 and ...♗h6.

Bill
Bill wants immediate action for a rook and suspects that 1...a4 is best. With the a-file likely to be his soon, life is looking rosy.

Chuck
Chuck definitely does not like the look of the ♗g5 pin that White could unleash at any moment. The precautionary 1...h6 both prevents this and introduces a serious idea of ...g6-g5 with reasonable chances for a kingside attack.

Debbie

What Black's position requires is a pawn break. One she had in mind was 1...c6, but now she thinks she'd prefer to employ her f-pawn on f5 instead. That means that now is the time to move her knight and she has opted for 1...♞e8, albeit narrowly over the also interesting 1...♞h5.

Eric

Eric favours completing his development with 1...♝d7. Then he will worry about how to activate his rooks, with ...♜b8, ...♛e8 and ...b7-b5 a realistic possibility to aid activity in that department.

□ Amy   □ Bill   □ Chuck   □ Debbie   □ Eric

Points: ....

White to play

A key factor in this ending is that the bishops are of opposite colour. Often – even with two pawns to the good – the attacker cannot
win. However, these connected pawns are quite advanced. What is
the best attempt that White can make to try and see one home?

Amy

Amy feels that the f-pawn is the most vulnerable of the two and
thus believes that White should begin with 1 f6. Then she will protect this pawn with her bishop, paving the way for g5-g6 to follow.

Bill

Bill prefers advancing his pawns on the opposite colour of his
bishop. Yes, after 1 g6+ he will be looking to get in f5-f6 and then
f6-f7 in the not too distant future.

Chuck

Chuck's long-term plan kicks off with 1 ♗d4. Then he will progress with g5-g6 followed by f5-f6. To make that final breakthrough f6-f7 he will manoeuvre his king around to e7 in order to prevent Black from trading his bishop for both pawns when the inevitable f6-f7 is played.

Debbie
Debbie feels that White has a variety of attempts to win but none will be successful provided Black continues to place his bishop on the best diagonal. This, of course, depends on where the white king goes.

Eric
The king is the key piece according to Eric, and he feels that White should take this opportunity to advance his king. After 1 ♔h7 he will have little difficulty escorting a pawn to glory.

☐ Amy   ☐ Bill   ☐ Chuck   ☐ Debbie   ☐ Eric

Points: ...10.........

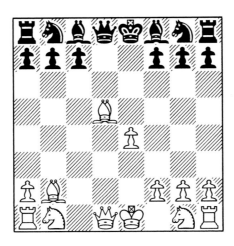

Black to play
The history of this position is that White has elected to gambit two
pawns to facilitate rapid development. Black has returned his d-
pawn, and the question is how should he attempt to nullify White's
remaining pressure?

Amy
Anxious to develop, Amy desires 1...♘f6 in order to gain a tempo on
White's light-squared bishop.

Bill
The most aggressive move according to Bill is 1...♗c5, homing in on
White's 'weak point' on f2. He will develop his king's knight next,
castle soon and eventually his extra pawn will prove decisive.

Chuck
Because Black is a pawn up Chuck likes 1...c6. After the bishop
moves Black can trade queens and things will be looking good for the

ending.

Debbie

Debbie considered the check 1...♗b4+ but decided on the safer 1...♗e7. If White responds with 2 ♗xg7 then 2...♗f6 should ensure that she doesn't ultimately finish the exchange down.

Eric

Eric has observed that White is threatening a big tactic and the only sensible way to avoid it is with 1...♕g5.

☐ Amy ☐ Bill ☐ Chuck ☐ Debbie ☐ Eric

Points: ....

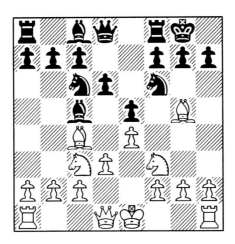

White to play
In this fairly symmetrical Italian Game position, what is White's best move, and why?

Amy
Amy proposes that, without doubt, 1 0-0 is the most accurate move. Opening principles include 'castling early' and that's just what she wants to do now.

Bill
Nothing so mundane from Bill who wants to jump in immediately with 1 ♘d5. Taking advantage of the bishop pin on the f6-knight, his plan should result in the doubling of black kingside pawns and an opportunity to generate an attack.

Chuck
Chuck prefers 1 ♗xf6. Although this concedes a bishop for a knight, the point is that 1...♕xf6 can then be met with 2 ♘d5. The

knight is superbly placed in the centre and the black queen is pretty much forced to retreat to her home square.

Debbie

Not entirely sure of how to continue (no great surprise there!), Debbie believes that she needs to begin actions on the queenside. She considers 1 a3 to be useful as it prevents a ....♝b4 pin and sets up the possibility of queenside expansion with 2 b4.

Eric

Eric suspects that White should be a little cautious. The useful 1 h3 prevents Black's own bishop from setting up an awkward pin with ....♝g4, and after castling White will have no serious worries about a back rank mate.

☐ Amy ☑ Bill ☐ Chuck ☐ Debbie ☐ Eric

Points: ....10....

White to play
Who is right about this seemingly straightforward ending?

Amy
White is easily winning according to Amy. Starting with 1 g4, and with 2 h4 to follow, the pawns will reach their destination without much difficulty.

Bill
Bill believes that this endgame is a draw. According to him Black will be able to give up his knight for the correct pawn after which White will be unable to win.

Chuck
Chuck feels that White should be winning fairly comfortably. He proposes 1 h3 so that he can follow with 2 g4 and then probably 3 g5. All White must do is avoid being left with a solitary h-pawn to partner his bishop.

Debbie
Debbie feels that White shouldn't move her pawns at all until White has managed to trade the knight for the bishop. It's going to be awkward but once the exchange has been made the rest will be easy.

Eric
Eric holds the view that White will win if he is careful. 1 ♗f3 looks like a good start and, if he can prevent Black from engineering a dark-squared blockade or sacrificing his knight for the g-pawn, then things will work out fine.

☐ Amy	☐ Bill	☐ Chuck	☐ Debbie	☐ Eric
Points:				

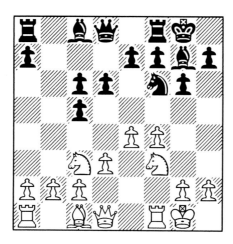

White to play

Entering the middlegame, can you suggest a suitable plan for White?

Amy

Amy is eager to develop her remaining bishop. She feels that it will be best placed fianchettoed on the queenside but acknowledges that with Black's bishop on g7 she must beware tactics. 1 ♕d2 is her idea, with b2-b3 and ♗b2 the intention.

Bill

Bill remembers that against the fianchettoed kingside it is good to advance your rook's pawn in a threatening manner. He has no hesitation whatsoever in launching it with 1 h4. His long-term plan is h4-h5, when he anticipates Black being in trouble on the h-file.

Chuck

Chuck also has a long-term plan to (hopefully) deliver checkmate.

His idea begins with 1 ♕e1, and he intends to swing the queen out to h4. Moves such as f4-f5 and ♗h6 might follow, when ♘g5 wouldn't leave him far from achieving his aim.

Debbie
Debbie remembers that making pawn breaks is a good thing to help activate rooks. At first she thought about pushing to b4, but available here and now is 1 d4. Since this also puts a pawn in the centre of the board it is her nomination.

Eric
Eric also wants to activate a rook and he sees the best opportunity as the half-open b-file. After 1 a4 he intends a rook swinger with ♖a3-b3. His view is that the kingside should be left alone for the time being.

☐ Amy	☐ Bill	☐ Chuck	☐ Debbie	☐ Eric
Points:				

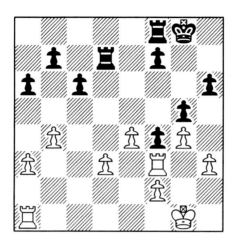

Black to play

It's Black to play in this double rook ending. Can you suggest an appropriate plan to help him on his way?

Amy

The black king should be centralised without any delay. The d4-square looks ripe for its occupation and g7-f6-e5 provides a suitable path.

Bill

Bill believes that by doubling his rooks now with 1...Rfd8 he can guarantee winning one of White's d- or e-pawns.

Chuck

Chuck has observed that White's rook is pretty much trapped on f3. He should begin hatching an evil plan to win it where it stands.

Debbie

Debbie feels that there are so many options for her rooks. As Black is worse due to the doubled f-pawns, she has come up with a sneaky sequence. After 1...♖fd8 2 ♖d1 ♖e8 (threatening the e-pawn thanks to the pin) 3 ♖e1 ♖ed8 4 ♖d1 she will soon be able to claim a draw by threefold repetition.

Eric

Fixing White's queenside pawns is what Eric has in mind. Yes, 1...b5 is his no.1 candidate, which stops White's queenside pawns in their tracks.

☐ Amy	☐ Bill	☐ Chuck	☐ Debbie	☐ Eric

Points: ....

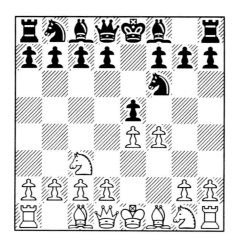

Black to play

White has just made an aggressive pawn thrust. How would you recommend that Black defends this position?

Amy

In order to keep a foothold in the centre Amy recommends 1...d6. This supports her attacked e5-pawn and enables her to continue her development.

Bill

Bill's view on this opening is that White has weakened himself along the b6-g1 diagonal and if Black can exploit this then he may be able to prevent his opponent from castling. The position calls for 1...♗c5.

Chuck

White has offered a gambit and Chuck can see no reason to decline it. After 1...exf4 Black could always return the extra pawn later, anyway.

Debbie

Debbie believes that although it is early in the game this is a critical moment for the second player. She believes that Black must respond actively with 1...d5, although she confesses that she is a little confused with the possible complications.

Eric

For Eric, supporting the centre and developing a piece will more than suffice. After 1...♘c6, in fact, Black will have more knights out than White.

☐ Amy	☐ Bill	☐ Chuck	☑ Debbie	☐ Eric

Points: ....

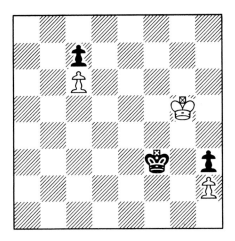

White to play
Yes, it's another king and pawn endgame! Get your counting hat on and tell us what should happen with best play. It is White to move.

Amy
The h3-pawn is by far the most dangerous of the pawns and so with 1 ♔h4 White should attempt to capture it as soon as possible. Once this is done White's h-pawn will deflect Black's monarch so that Black's c-pawn can be won and a promotion will take place on c8.

Bill
With 1 ♔f5 or 1 ♔f6 White must head immediately to capture the c7-pawn. Black will snare the h2-pawn, but White will queen first and win.

Chuck
Chuck believes that Bill's plan is the only option but has counted that Black is ahead in the race for promotion. However, Black will

queen and White will then merely push his pawn to the seventh rank, when the position is still a draw.

Debbie

Plenty of agreement here, then! Debbie appears to have analysed like Chuck but her final conclusion is that Black will win as a queen always beats a pawn on the seventh rank. It is a lengthy process but essentially the queen forces the king in front of the pawn and that provides time for the attacking king to return. The routine is repeated until the pawn is captured and/or mate delivered.

Eric

Eric has calculated that White loses in the pawn capturing race. However, an alternative plan exists in waiting for the black king to capture on h2 and then boxing it in with ♔f2. As it won't be able to escape, a draw will be the outcome, either through repetition or stalemate.

☐ Amy   ☐ Bill   ☐ Chuck   ☐ Debbie   ☐ Eric

Points: ....

White to play
It is White to move but his rook is in a fairly passive position here and his king is nowhere to be seen. Is there any hope of getting anything out of this game?

Amy
Yes, White can draw but only if the king is returned to action as quickly as possible. It is no surprise, then, that Amy recommends the immediate 1 ♔b7.

Bill
Bill's startling view is that Black is not even genuinely threatening to win provided the white king does not make an early appearance on the b-file. With 1 ♔a7 White will have no trouble holding the draw.

Chuck
Rooks belong behind passed pawns and, adhering to this principle, Chuck advocates 1 ♖e8, from where it can get behind either the b-

pawn or the g-pawn.

Debbie
Debbie feels that this is a rare instance where blocking the pawns is a good idea. After 1 ♖g1 it is difficult for Black to make progress and, indeed, only if the enemy king threatens to come to f2 should the rook move again (this time to b1).

Eric
Eric believes that the white rook must maximise its potential. After 1 ♖e3+ the rook should transfer to behind the b-pawn. Eventually a queen versus rook endgame will result with White having reasonable drawing chances.

☐ Amy   ☐ Bill   ☐ Chuck   ☐ Debbie ☐ Eric

Points: ....

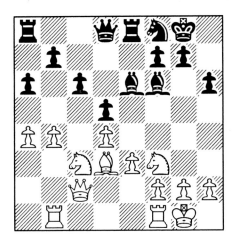

White to play
In this middlegame (resulting from a Queen's Gambit opening) how might you advise White to continue?

Amy
According to Amy, definitely with 1 b5. This is often the sort of move that White strives for in this opening, and a pawn break should lead to some serious rook action.

Bill
Bill feels that 1 h3 is a useful multi-purpose move. It prevents Black from playing 1...♗g4 and, secondly, depending on how the second player responds, White can seriously contemplate a kingside offensive starting with the thrust of the g-pawn.

Chuck
Chuck recommends the immediate 1 e4. It puts a pawn in the centre and, if taken, opens up the position nicely for the white knights.

Debbie

Having developed her minor pieces nicely, Debbie wants to allocate her rooks satisfactory squares, too. She believes in centralisation and has opted for 1 ♖fe1, with ♖bd1 likely to follow soon.

Eric

Eric wants to squeeze his opponent. A bind can be set up on the queenside with 1 a5, when the c3-knight will then have some useful options. After ♘a4 it can choose between homes on c5 and b6.

| ☐ Amy | ☐ Bill | ☐ Chuck | ☐ Debbie | ☐ Eric |

Points: ....

White to play

White to play must treasure his remaining pawn if he is to win this limited material endgame. Is this realistic and, if so, what are his chances of winning?

Amy

Not good. Amy's experience is that knights are tricky pieces and the black steed will be able to sacrifice itself for the currently blockaded a-pawn. With just a king and bishop versus king remaining the game will be declared a draw.

Bill

Bill wants to attack – too much talking and not enough action! Being careful to avoid forks, White's king can advance toward the knight which might find itself trapped by the king and bishop.

Chuck

The game is a draw according to Chuck, but for one reason only.

White has the wrong coloured bishop for the queening square of the a-pawn. Black will be able to give up his knight for nothing at the right time and still White will be unable to convert the full point.

Debbie
Debbie hesitated over this one, which she considers to be one of the most difficult questions thus far. Her non-committal answer is that it could go either way (excluding, that is, a Black win!).

Eric
Eric became quite excited about this one. He has concluded that there is an excellent defence involving the black knight setting up camp in the corner. Black then retreats his own king and boxes in the White's on a8. Unable to escape, a draw will be the outcome.

☐ Amy   ☐ Bill   ☐ Chuck   ☐ Debbie   ☐ Eric

Points: ....

White/Black to play

Who has the correct view about this clearly staged but nevertheless thought-provoking endgame?

Amy

Amy believes that, whoever is to move, the position is a draw. There
is no way that the knight will be able to control the relevant
squares that in turn prevent the white king from escaping its cage.

Bill

Bill concludes that White is winning whoever is to move. A bishop
would have no trouble controlling a vital square and nor will a knight.
It is a long way from the action now but, given time, the knight will
have a serious impact.

Chuck

Chuck has completed his analysis and has concluded that if it is
White to play then he is winning, but if it is Black to play, provided

the black king continues to oscillate between c7 and c8, the game will be drawn.

Debbie

Debbie got a headache studying this one. She definitely believes that the outcome is dependent upon who is to move, but had to check it over and over again. Her conclusion is that White can realistically expect to win only if it is Black to play.

Eric

Eric has studied the laws of chess well and remembers reading that this position is a draw because fifty moves will pass without a pawn being moved or a piece being taken. Were this limit extended to a hundred moves, then White would be able to win.

☐ Amy   ☐ Bill   ☐ Chuck   ☑ Debbie   ☐ Eric

Points: ...10....

White to play
There's not much left in this king and pawn ending in which it is White to play. What should be the result with best play, and what is your reasoning?

Amy
It is a draw according to Amy because the white king is behind the more advanced of the two pawns. In order to help in its promotion the king needs to be in front of the pawn, and to obtain what is known as the 'opposition'.

Bill
The position is a trivial win for White according to Bill, who advocates stepping his king out of the way and advancing his two pawns in tandem. The black king will run out of squares and a promotion will result.

Chuck

Chuck suggests that White can win simply by advancing his king and the furthermost pawn up the board. His implication, though, is that the second pawn is vital in that it is required to shed a tempo.

Debbie

Trying to recall some of her endgame theory, Debbie has put forward a completely different conclusion. The endgame is drawn but has nothing to do with the amount of pawns on the file. The key feature is that it is a knight's file. If the king cannot get in front of the pawn, then only a centre pawn (including bishop's) will win.

Eric

Eric's offering is that the second (i.e. rear) pawn has been placed in this puzzle as a red herring. With or without it White can advance slowly and have absolutely no problem queening. However, the more pawns, the more queens!

□ Amy   □ Bill   ☑ Chuck   □ Debbie   □ Eric

Points: ....

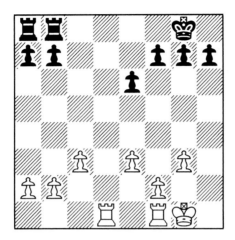

White to play

The material is level in this double rook ending. How would you suggest that White should tackle the position?

Amy

With 1 ♔g2 (possibly intending ♔f3-e4) White should start to centralise her king. This is a universal plan in endgames as the king is a valuable piece.

Bill

Whilst Black's main forces are concentrated on the queenside White should take advantage on the other side of the board. A kingside attack won't necessarily be successful with so many pieces already exchanged, but an expansion with, for example, 1 f4 (and g4-g5) can only be useful.

Chuck

Centralising the rooks is Chuck's plan. Not with 1 ♖fe1, which clearly achieves little, but rather 1 ♖d4. The rook is flexible here and White can always double rooks to dominate what is, after all, the only open file on the board.

Debbie
White's pawn majority is on the queenside. Debbie wanted to do something with the pawns over there and eventually recommends 1 a4 to remind Black that he must remain defensive.

Eric
'Rook's love the seventh rank' is what Eric is going by, and after 1 ♖d7 his ultimate plan is to go a step further by doubling first on the d-file and then, given half the chance, the seventh rank. Imagine having one rook on c7 and one on d7. The hoovering that could be done!

☐ Amy	☐ Bill	☐ Chuck	☐ Debbie	☐ Eric

Points: ....2........

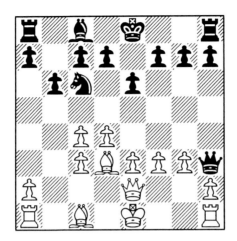

Black to play

It's Black to play. Can you suggest a weakness or two that he might wish to concentrate on when considering a middlegame plan?

Amy

Yes, the black queen is offside and in serious danger. Black should play 1...d6 and, with the coincidentally challenging ...e6-e5, he will have secured a safe return for it along the h3-d7 diagonal.

Bill

White will regret having a pawn on g3. The black queen is already ingrained in White's kingside. A plan of 1...h5, intending ...h5-h4 to activate the rook, should really do some damage.

Chuck

Hardly a cheeky or sneaky suggestion from Chuck this time. Observing that White is preparing to play ♗a3, he wants to play 1...0-0 now. Following this he will get organised on the queenside by ultimately arranging the break with his b-pawn.

mately arranging the break with his b-pawn.

Debbie

Debbie suggests that White's doubled c-pawns are a weakness and the one on c4 is the most vulnerable. She can't decide if she would rather win it or make the square an outpost. 1...♗a6 is her preference, with ...♘a5 and possibly even ...d7-d5 to follow.

Eric

Completing development is a priority for Eric. He wants to castle (whichever side is allowed) very soon but before that comes the obvious 1...♗b7. He has highlighted White's f3-pawn as a big target.

☐ Amy   ☐ Bill   ☐ Chuck   ☐ Debbie   ☑ Eric

Points: ....

White to play

White is to move in this queen versus pawns ending. Who provides the most accurate assessment of the position?

Amy

Amy feels that because the white king is so far away White will be unable to win but can, of course, draw in any number of ways.

Bill

Bill can't see what all the fuss is about. As far as he's concerned White will have little trouble winning and he has precious little to add.

Chuck

Ironically, Chuck observes that were Black's pawn already on h2 then the presence of an a-pawn would be detrimental. Alas it is not, so Black can jettison his a-pawn to secure the draw.

Debbie

Debbie remembers that a queen versus a rook's pawn on the seventh rank is a draw if the attacker's king is a fair distance away and the defending king close by (and preventing the queen from setting up residence on the queening square). However, the presence of two rook's pawns has confused her, with her eventual conclusion being that one compensates the other. It should be a draw with best play.

Eric

1 ♕g8+ ♔f2 2 ♕a2+ ♔g1 3 ♕xa4 is one way to begin when, after 3...h2, White will be able to force the king in front of the h-pawn repeatedly to buy the required time to recall his own monarch to active duty. This is a process that this book has seen already, and White wins comfortably.

☐ Amy ☐ Bill ☐ Chuck ☐ Debbie ☐ Eric

Points: ....

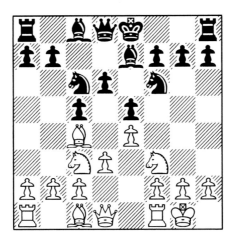

White to play
With development nearly complete and the middlegame almost here, how would you advise White to continue?

Amy
White must play 1 &b5 now, i.e. before Black castles. The c6-knight will be pinned, which means that it won't get to hop into d4. After trading the bishop for it, either the outpost on d5 will remain or Black will receive doubled pawns.

Bill
Bill likes the look of 1 ♘g5. The only way for Black to sensibly defend the weak point on f7 is with 1...0-0 or 1...♖f8. Then after 2 ♘xf7 ♖xf7 3 &xf7+ ♔xf7 White will have an encouraging position. The material situation will be equal (having traded 6 points for 6 points) but the black king will have been exposed.

Chuck

Chuck also feels that 1 ♘g5 is justified but his idea is that after Black castles he can get in the pawn break 2 f4.

Debbie

Debbie has so many moves that she wants to play. Preventing a ...♗g4 pin with 1 h3 is a good start, after which completing development with, for example, ♗d2 and ♖e1 should follow.

Eric

Eric feels that something should be made of the outpost on d5. He had an idea of 1 ♗g5 in order to first trade his bishop for the f6-knight, but then decided to propose the immediate 1 ♘d5.

□ Amy	□ Bill	□ Chuck	□ Debbie	☑ Eric
Points: ..4..........				

76

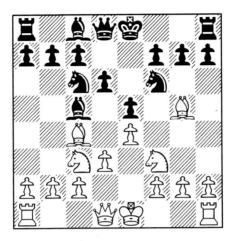

Black to play

In this apparently uninspirational Symmetrical Italian Game position, can you offer a suggestion as to how Black should deal with the threat of ♘d5?

Amy

Amy is anxious to castle. She feels that her king is more exposed the longer it stays in the centre.

Bill

Bill likes the continuation 1...h6 2 ♗h4 g5 3 ♗g3 ♗g4. Then White has to deal with a similar threat of ...♘d4, while, rather than castling kingside, Black can consider moving the queen and castling long.

Chuck

Chuck feels that the best way to deal with this situation is to rule out ♘d5. The best way to do this is with 1...♗b4, pinning the c3-knight and introducing the possibility of doubling White's pawns.

Debbie

Debbie is so often caught between two or three moves but this time she is convinced by one move that performs two or three functions! Yes, 1...♘e7 unpins the f6-knight, controls the d5-square and, additionally, the transfer ...♘g6 might also prove useful.

Eric

Eric feels that Black cannot go wrong by maintaining the symmetry. After 1...♗g4 2 ♘d5 ♘d4 the game should end in a draw, but this is anyway a good result for Black.

☐ Amy   ☐ Bill   ☑ Chuck   ☐ Debbie   ☐ Eric

Points: ....

White to play

The black pawn is just one square away from promotion but it is White to play. This is a tactical endgame. What should happen?

Amy

Obviously White does not want Black crowning a new queen. Amy feels that 1 ♖a8, 1 ♖h1 and 1 ♖h2+ are all fine with the rook soon being traded for the pawn.

Bill

Bill has an amazing idea for White to try for the full point, being attracted to 1 ♖h2+ ♚b1 2 ♔a3. Black can have his new queen but will lose nonetheless, as he cannot prevent ♖h1+ in any satisfactory manner.

Chuck

Chuck likes 1 ♖h2+ ♚b1 2 ♔b3, since whatever Black promotes to White will win by force.

Debbie

Debbie feels that the error that others in the panel have made here is in forgetting about under-promotion. There is no obligation to turn a pawn into a queen, and Black will be saved should White get ambitious.

Eric

The most precise move order according to Eric is 1 ♖h2+ ♔b1 2 ♖h1+ ♔b2 3 ♖h2+ ♔b1 4 ♖h1+ ♔b2, when White can announce that he will play 5 ♖h2+ with a three-fold repetition.

☐ Amy   ☑ Bill   ☐ Chuck   ☐ Debbie   ☐ Eric

Points: ....

White to play
The white king is seriously out of position! But can White (to play)
work a miracle and win this game?

Amy
Yes, but he must act quickly. 1 ♖a6+ is correct according to Amy,
who sees the checks that will be given along the ranks as an integral
part of enabling White's king to have a critical influence on the proceedings.

Bill
Bill's surprise choice is 1 ♖a7. He feels that it is vital that the rook
gets behind the passed pawn. The black king will have to advance to
make any progress and then the white king will be freed to make its
necessary contribution.

Chuck
Chuck wants to prevent the black king from advancing and thus fa-

vours cutting it off with 1 ♖a5. He feels that the white king is required to ultimately help round up the pawn, but that it will have
plenty of time to make a reappearance on the scene.

Debbie
Debbie has analysed 1 ♖a2 and 1 ♖a3 and has concluded that unless
Black were to volunteer some mistakes, only the former will win her
the game.

Eric
Clearly all of our panel think that White is winning but Eric's view is
that the accurate move is 1 ♖a1. The pawn will frustratingly be
halted at the last post as the white king retreats just in time.

☐ Amy   ☐ Bill   ☐ Chuck   ☐ Debbie   ☐ Eric

Points: ....

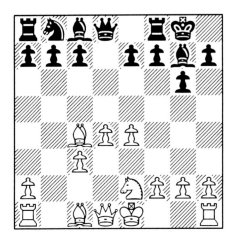

Black to play
White has emerged from the opening with an attractive pawn centre. Is it worth Black doing anything about this?

Amy
Amy's view is that perhaps Black should attack the centre later, but
certainly not just yet. Instead she prefers concentrating on completing her development. There are no good options for the light-
squared bishop along the c8-h3 diagonal, so Amy proposes the fi-
anchetto after 1...b6.

Bill
Bill thinks that Black should react to White's premature centre play
with action on the wings. 1...h6 is just the ticket, with 2...g5 next on
the agenda.

Chuck
Although Chuck does want to develop the queenside pieces soon, he

also wants to pressurise White's centre, too. His interesting choice is 1...♚h8, which unpins the f7-pawn with which Black can then strike.

Debbie
Debbie is all for attacking the white centre immediately. Initially she dwelt on 1...e5 but now feels that her e-pawn is too valuable. Finally clear in her mind, her nomination is 1...c5.

Eric
Eric believes that it is a little risky to challenge the centre at this early stage. He would rather contain it by taking a grip on the d5-square. 1...c6 is his favourite, with ...e7-e6 to follow when necessary.

☐ Amy   ☐ Bill   ☐ Chuck   ☐ Debbie   ☐ Eric

Points: ....

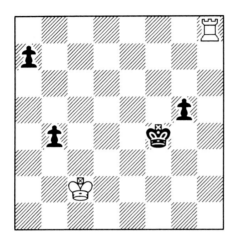

White to play
Obviously White, to play, would hate to lose this position but is really trying to win. Which of these suggested moves/plans make sense for White?

Amy
White should start with 1 ♔d2 or, perhaps, 1 ♔d3. The white king is best positioned in close proximity to its opposite number while the rook can set about collecting Black's kingside pawns.

Bill
There is no time to be lost, according to Bill. The rook can monitor the progress of Black's g-pawn and as it is already over there the white king should get to grips with the terrible twosome. 1 ♔b3 is his starting choice.

Chuck
Chuck again feels that this is a good opportunity to cut off the

black king, and after 1 ♖h3 the king will be prevented from advancing. The rook will provide a good barrier to hinder the black pawns as they approach their sixth rank and the white king should return to the kingside.

Debbie
Debbie can't quite decide on which way to commit her king, so she wants to go after the b-pawn with her rook. 1 ♖b8 is how she would like to begin, and she will decide on her monarch later.

Eric
Eric's analysis runs 1 ♖a8 g4 2 ♖xa7 g3 3 ♖a4. He picks up the b-pawn and then the g-pawn should easily be negotiated.

☐ Amy   ☐ Bill   ☐ Chuck   ☐ Debbie   ☐ Eric

Points: ....

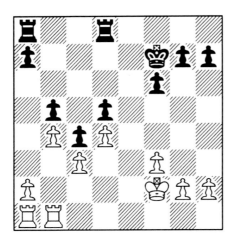

White to play
What is the best plan for White in this even looking double rook ending?

Amy
According to Amy, taking control of the solitary open file should be a priority. After 1 ℤe1 White should be prepared to double rooks on the e-file.

Bill
Bill believes that there is little future for the white rooks on the queenside. The 'entry points' on the e-file also appear to be adequately protected. Therefore he proposes advancing his kingside pawns and, hopefully, using his rooks in this sector.

Chuck
Chuck likes 1 a4. His view is that 1...a6 is pretty forced, when the sequence 2 axb5 axb5 3 ℤxa8 ℤxa8 4 ℤe1 will see him having taken

a stance on the a-file in order to take control of the e-file.

Debbie
Debbie feels that Black's space advantage provides him with a very minimal edge. To guarantee a draw Debbie advocates the sequence 1 a4 a6 2 a5. With the queenside sealed off, the likelihood is that the rooks will be traded on the e-file and the point shared.

Eric
Eric has seen this sort of thing before and believes that White holds the upper hand in view of the tension on the a-file. He proposes 1 a4 and, after 1...a6, the sneaky 2 ♖a3. It is possible to double rooks only while the pawns offer cover there, and the likely result is White being able to infiltrate the a-file with a rook or two.

☐ Amy   ☐ Bill   ☐ Chuck   ☐ Debbie   ☐ Eric

Points: ....

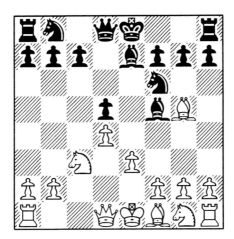

White to play
What do you recommend as being White's most precise method of treating this position?

Amy
Nothing spectacular. White should start with 1 ♘f3, when 2 ♗e2 and 3 0-0 should follow. Amy believes that White's priority should be the completion of development.

Bill
As Black spurned the opportunity to castle last turn, Bill wants to make him pay with 1 ♗b5+. His logic is that Black will either be forced to set up a self-pin or else weaken his pawn structure with 1...c6.

Chuck
Chuck thinks that he can see a way to win a pawn. The move ♕b3 hits both b7 and d5 and, after inserting 1 ♗xf6 ♗xf6, he believes

that there is no satisfactory way for Black to defend.

Debbie
Debbie is not quite sure how to develop her kingside pieces. Her decision is to defer that problem for the moment in favour of 1 ♖c1. After all, although it's not clear where the other pieces should be, the rook definitely desires the half-open file.

Eric
Eric sees Black's light-squared bishop as occupying an annoying diagonal. He feels it is necessary to neutralise it with 1 ♗d3. Following this, the king's knight will have the option of sliding to e2 as well as the more traditional f3-square.

☐ Amy ☐ Bill ☐ Chuck ☐ Debbie ☐ Eric

Points: ....

White to play

There's not much left on the board but with White to play, what should be the outcome of this king and pawn ending?

Amy

Amy feels that the white king should advance towards the enemy pawns. After 1 ♔c5 she believes that White will pick up both pawns, thus easily promoting a pawn.

Bill

Unusual subtlety from Bill! He prefers 1 ♔d5, gaining the 'opposition', when the black king will be pushed away from protecting his pawns. White will win.

Chuck

Chuck acknowledges that 1 ♔d5 is the best attempt but, alas, feels that the position is anyway drawn. The problem will come after his king captures the a6-pawn, as Black's king will be able to box it in on the a-file, resulting in either a draw by repetition or stalemate.

Debbie
Debbie got a little confused in her calculations but eventually decided that 1 ♔e5 is the correct way to start the proceedings. Her opinion is that the black king will be unable to prevent its opposite number from slowly but surely picking off the pawns.

Eric
It is just a draw according to Eric, who believes that this 'opposition' stuff is nonsense. How either side can realistically expect to win with so few pieces around is beyond him. As White he would safely retreat with 1 ♔c3 and accompany it with a draw offer.

☐ Amy   ☐ Bill   ☐ Chuck   ☐ Debbie   ☐ Eric

Points: ....

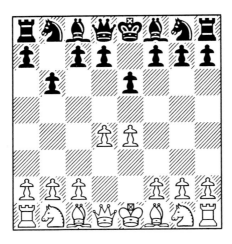

White to play

Surely this is the easiest question in the book as, after all, only two moves each have been made. There may appear to be several sensible moves here for White, but which is the most accurate of our characters' offerings, and why?

Amy

Amy definitely likes 1 ♘c3. The general opening principal that she likes to adhere to is 'knights before bishops'. By developing this knight she is also defending the soon to be attacked e4-pawn.

Bill

Having been forced to answer lots of questions, Bill has come to realise just how important the concept of a 'pawn break' is. He would like to play 1 a4 now, not with the beginner's ♖a3 in mind, but rather a4-a5, which should create a half-open file for his rook.

Chuck

Chuck spots a good opportunity to hold a black centre pawn in place. 1 ♗b5 pins the d7-pawn whilst usefully developing a piece.

Debbie

Debbie feels that the only obvious pieces to commit here are knights. Though contemplating 1 ♘c3, she has instead opted for 1 ♘f3 as she anticipates castling kingside.

Eric

As far as Eric is concerned, he has a nice pawn centre and it is imperative that he supports it. 1 ♗e3 protects d4 and offers the b1-knight the chance to slip into d2.

☐ Amy   ☐ Bill   ☐ Chuck   ☐ Debbie   ☐ Eric

Points: ....

White to play
It is White to play. Who has the right story about this tricky king
and pawn ending?

Amy
Amy would like to involve her king but it is clearly caged in. Consequently the result will definitely be a draw.

Bill
Bill believes that by sacrificing the f-pawn now with 1 f5 White will
be able to obtain the opposition. He will win Black's g4-pawn and
then use his king to usher his own pawn home.

Chuck
Chuck has a very devious idea. He acknowledges that the black king
will stubbornly refuse to let White's escape the back rank. However, he has observed a kind of blind spot. The king can be mirrored
all the way over to b8 but, after ♔a8, Black cannot play ...♔a6 be-

cause he would be outside the range of stopping the passed pawn. Essentially, then, White's king will trawl the sides of the board until it can return to the action; once there it will nudge the black king away to win the black g-pawn and thus the game.

Debbie

Debbie is happy that she, too, followed Chuck's line of thinking. However, she believes that she has discovered a flaw. At the end of it all White will not be able to win the g-pawn or promote a pawn as Black will obtain the opposition.

Eric

Eric finds these answers laughable. He believes that the others have missed that Black can draw (or indeed win in Bill's case) by advancing his own king and capturing White's g3-pawn.

☐ Amy   ☐ Bill   ☐ Chuck   ☐ Debbie   ☐ Eric

Points: ....

White to play
With White to play, does he have any hope?

Amy
Yes. Amy thinks that this is a draw, but only if the white rook leaves the danger area – her view is that it would be better off on, for example, b8. In fact she has recommended 1 ♖b8 as being the best way to begin.

Bill
Although Bill acknowledges that, generally, a queen will defeat a rook, here he thinks that White can draw through tactical means.

Chuck
Chuck has spotted 1 ♖b3+. He will win the queen or else the rook will be captured and it will be stalemate.

Debbie

Debbie seems to recall (but she's not certain!) that unless there is an immediate tactic that wins the queen, a king and queen will always defeat a king and rook. There is a four point material advantage there, after all, and so it is no great surprise that here, just like in the majority of times, Black is winning.

Eric

Eric's view is – providing that White is sensible and keeps his rook close to his king – White should be able to hold the draw. He advocates 1 ♖c2, after which White's fortress will be difficult to break down.

☐ Amy	☐ Bill	☐ Chuck	☐ Debbie	☐ Eric

Points: ....

White to play
With best play can White, to move, possibly win this position? Select the most appropriate answer.

Amy
Amy sees the position as an easy win. With 1 ♔e6 the king will win
the race to capture the h6-pawn, after which White's own pawn will
promote with the black king too far away.

Bill
Bill, in contrast to Amy, believes that the position is a draw. Obvi-
ously White should go for the h6-pawn, but Bill's counting has
White's king boxed in by its opposite number.

Chuck
Chuck has a sneaky 'shielding off' technique in mind. His analysis
runs 1 ♔e5 ♚g3 2 ♔f5, when Black's king has been prevented from
returning to hinder White's, while 2...♚h4 3 ♔g6 is obviously of no

use to the defender.

Debbie

Debbie feels that the position is a draw, but only because the remaining pawn is a rook's pawn. Although White will be able to obtain the opposition at a critical stage, this will not be sufficient to help her pawn through to promotion.

Eric

Eric appears, at least temporarily, to have altered his views on the ability to win with limited material. He suggests that White can win but only by making the most of his king with 1 ♔e4.

☐ Amy   ☐ Bill   ☐ Chuck   ☐ Debbie ☐ Eric

Points: ....

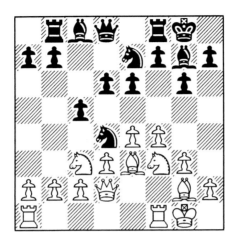

White to play
Black has a well-placed knight in this tense middlegame struggle.
What might be a suitable way for White to deal with this situation?

Amy
Amy believes that the knight has to go and there is no reason to
hesitate. It is worth trading it for one of her own knights – hence
the simple 1 ♘xd4.

Bill
Bill is not too worried by the presence of the knight and he believes
that he can play around it. His view is that he has an initiative on
the kingside, and 1 f5 is just the sort of aggressive continuation
that he likes. The f-pawn could be a real thorn in Black's camp and it
is a pawn break that may see some action for a rook or two on the
f-file.

Chuck

Chuck wants to force the knight away with a pawn. His nomination is the temporary withdrawal 1 ♘d1, making way for c2-c3.

Debbie

Debbie would also like to have the option of c2-c3 but can't quite decide on where to move her knight. Eventually she committed herself to 1 ♘e2 because it pressurises the knight directly.

Eric

Eric agrees that Black's central knight must be evicted but he views withdrawing the c3-knight as too time-consuming. Capturing with the f3-knight is tactically flawed but he can see nothing wrong with 1 ♗xd4. Upon the expected 1...cxd4 he will play 2 ♘e2, hitting the d4-pawn and ready to begin operations on the kingside.

☐ Amy   ☐ Bill   ☐ Chuck   ☐ Debbie ☐ Eric

Points: ....

White to play
White has the enemy king tied down but how can he finish him off?

Amy
Amy's suggestion is to seek a back rank mate as soon as possible, her recommendation being 1 ♖h1. Upon 1...♗e6 2 ♖h8+ ♗c8, White then wins with a passing move such as 3 ♖g8.

Bill
Bill is thinking along the same lines as Amy but proposes 1 ♖f1.

Chuck
Chuck's opinion is that White cannot win because Black has got his defence just right. The black bishop cannot allow the rook to gain a vital tempo in order to get to the back rank, so it has wisely positioned itself in the correct corner of the board.

Debbie

Debbie is confused because – provided the rook is safe – she thought that king and rook always defeat king and bishop. She favours 1 ♖c7 when, with the black king still locked in, White will eventually win.

Eric

Eric suddenly sprung to life with this question. He proposes 1 ♖c2 and the concept of harassing the bishop and chasing it out into the open. His ultimate aim is to obtain that vital tempo that will see the rook reach the back rank without Black's king having an opportunity to move.

☐ Amy	☐ Bill	☐ Chuck	☐ Debbie	☐ Eric

Points: ....

White to play
Returning to basics, is this king and pawn situation as simple as it looks? Which of our panel is most in tune with the situation?

Amy
Yes, it is a simple win for White according to Amy. She believes 1 g6+ is correct and, after 1...♔g8 2 g7 ♔h7, observes that 3 ♔f7 will see the pawn home.

Bill
Bill thinks that White is easily winning but that the king must advance first in order to support the pawn. 1 ♔f7 ♔h8 2 g6 will suffice.

Chuck
Chuck recognises this as an exception to the traditional king and pawn versus king scenario. The game is drawn thanks to some critical stalemate themes available to Black.

Debbie

Debbie recalls being told in an earlier puzzle that if the king makes it to the sixth rank in front of the pawn, then the attacker wins, whoever is to move. As this can be arranged her assessment is that White wins.

Eric

Eric's opinion is that 1 ♔f5 is the best practical try. There will be no stalemate problems if White is careful and he can advance his pawn to the end of the board at his leisure. The position is a straightforward win for White.

☐ Amy   ☐ Bill   ☐ Chuck   ☐ Debbie   ☐ Eric

Points: ....

Solutions To Test One

Solution 1-1

White does have a nice pawn structure in the centre which could be very useful for cramping his opponent. Both Amy and Eric suggest sensible moves, although not ones that get to the crux of the situation. The only offering that gives Black the opportunity to claim a fair share of territory is Debbie's:
1...d5 2 exd5 ♞xd5

(see following diagram)

Black's knights are reasonably placed, the d-pawn is nicely blockaded and the once troublesome white e-pawn is no more. Possibly achieving a similar result was her other intriguing idea of 1...♞xe4, and she is definitely deserving of full marks.

I am not convinced by Chuck's recommendation. There is not even a bishop ready to pin the f6-knight on g5, it's rather early to be worrying about back rank mates and h7 wouldn't be the most comfortable square for a knight.

As for Bill, his ramblings are simply preposterous. With an army of pieces we do not use only one. He might dream of being able to checkmate White down the h-file but this is indeed a dream!

Points

Amy	3
Bill	0
Chuck	0
Debbie	10
Eric	3

Solution 1-2

It is wrong to advance the f-pawn until the white rook is in its optimum position. Indeed it is worth noting that 1 f7? allows the cheeky 1...♖e6+ 2 ♖xe6 stalemate! Chuck noticed this and indeed 1 ♖a7 ♖d8 (the rook cannot leave the back rank due to 2 ♖a8+) 2 ♖h7 is clearly the best suggestion.

Black's rook is in no position to stop ♖h8+ and only after 2...♔g8 would we see 3 f7+ ♔f8 4 ♖h8+ ♔e7 5 ♖xd8 when the pawn promotes. Note that with the pawn on f6 White's king is protected against

an annoying check on the sixth rank, and the king and pawn are superbly positioned to keep the rook in a passive role. Even if successful, Eric's elaborate plan would only leave his king too far away to protect his pawn, and Debbie must learn to be less gullible. You may hear plenty of adages such as 'a pawn is a pawn' – Grandmasters might use this in order to justify analysis! Each position, of course, should be taken on its own merits.

Points

Amy	0
Bill	1
Chuck	10
Debbie	0
Eric	0

Solution 1-3

I am afraid that Debbie has been blinded by science again but I do have a certain amount of sympathy for Eric. Everything about his summary holds true until the 'game over' bit. Examining 1 cxd6 ♔xd6 2

♔e3 ♚d5 3 g4 ♚e5 4 g5 ♚f5 5 g6 ♚xg6 6 ♚xe4 ♚f6 7 ♚d5 it can be seen that Black's king is, in fact, spoilt for choice. First, it can hastily retreat to the a8-corner where, because we have only a rook's pawn, White will be unable to promote. Alternatively, he can follow the white king to keep it boxed in on the a-file. Provided he doesn't allow the white king to aid in the pawn's advance by getting to b7, Black will be fine.

Chuck is absolutely right. A little calculation shows that taking the Bill route enables Black to capture the c-pawn and still get back in time to prevent the g-pawn from promoting. However, 1 c6 ♚e6 2 g4 d5 3 g5 is a nightmare scenario for Black.

The isolated white pawns tease Black's king because approaching one allows the other to advance. Chuck is right to be wary of Black's pawns. With any major pieces present those black centre pawns would be a lot more dangerous, but here White's king can easily watch over them.

One drawback with Amy's suggestion is that after, for example, 1 ♚e3 dxc5 2 g4 c4, Black's isolated pawns will soon be immune to capture for fear of one of them promoting.

Points

Amy	0
Bill	1
Chuck	10
Debbie	0
Eric	2

Solution 1-4

If you didn't select Bill's choice then there is an important lesson here. However many general principles or however much opening theory you may know, you should make sure not to get blinded by science!

Black is offering a free pawn here, and the fact that he will get a slight development advantage after 1 dxc6 ♘xc6 is not going to win him any 'Gambit of the Year' awards.

Take a look at 1 e4 d5 2 exd5 ♘f6
3 c4 c6 4 dxc6?! ♘xc6

Debbie   1
Eric   3

Here White regrets having a pawn on c4 as now the d4-square is a potentially important outpost for Black, whose pieces will flood into play with ...e7-e5 and ...♗c5, and even f2 may come under pressure with White unlikely to ever be in a position to push his pawn to d4.

However, this is different to our initial position, where Black's offering is completely unjustified. Amy's suggestion is flawed in that 1...cxd5 will force her bishop to move, whilst 1 ♘f3 is more logical than 1 ♘c3 as White is more likely to castle kingside (and should thus give preference to developing kingside pieces).

Eric's option is acceptable but one should not look a gift horse in the mouth!

Points

Amy	0
Bill	10
Chuck	1

Fortunately for Amy I don't award negative marks! Okay, running completely out of pawns may be somewhat unfortunate (as one can't checkmate with king and bishop or knight against king), but with pieces on the board they are more easily preserved.

I definitely recommend you trying the different permutations for yourself. Black would experience no joy with his h-pawns and so his king must head straight for White's queenside pawns. Unlike a bishop, you will notice how a knight does not look after pawns too well (nor indeed do they safely protect a knight!).

The light-squared bishop cannot attack pawns on dark squares but it can prevent the enemy king from defending them while White's king goes on the offensive. Eric is absolutely right.

Points

Amy	0
Bill	0
Chuck	0
Debbie	5
Eric	10

Solution 1-6

I must say here that with the exception of poor Amy, all of the offerings were plausible. Although Debbie and Eric's bishop and rook moves are very reasonable, there isn't any need to commit them just yet. It is worth remembering that there is a difference between moving a piece and developing a piece.

I am very attracted to Chuck's plan, which makes excellent use of White's space advantage. Indeed the only thing that betters that is the application of a 'Greek' gift with 1 ♗xh7+ ♚xh7 2 ♘g5+

(see following diagram)

Black faces an unpleasant decision here. Retreating the king is grim, e.g. 2...♚g8 3 ♕h5 ♖e8 4 ♕xf7+ ♚h8 5 ♕h5+ ♚g8 6 ♕h7+

♚f8 7 ♕h8 ♚e7 8 ♕xg7 mate. There would, of course, be a choice of tasty discovered checks after 2...♚h6 and, when analysing this typical sacrifice over the board, the acid test usually comes with 2...♚g6. Then placing the white queen on the g-file should be considered, but here a convincing continuation is 3 ♕d3+ f5 4 exf6+ ♚xf6 5 ♕f3+ ♚g6 6 ♕e4+. Black then either gets mated or drops a rook after 6...♖f5 7 g4. Note the importance here of the absence of Black's dark-squared bishop.

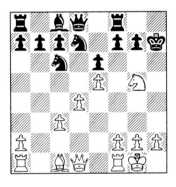

Certainly Black has played passively and should probably have used his c-pawn to strike out at White's centre. However, had his bishop have been on e7 rather than traded off for White's knight, then the whole combination would not have worked. I am not going to categorically say that bishops are better than knights, but one should think very carefully of the implications before casually engaging in an exchange. Amy, take note!

Points

Amy	0
Bill	10
Chuck	6
Debbie	3
Eric	3

Solution 1-7

There is an important stalemate theme here that can be observed by taking a look at the position below.

The black king has camped in the corner and continues to alternate between a8 and b7. Ideally White would like to defend the pawn with his king and manoeuvre his knight to flush out Black's king (or deliver checkmate). Alas, any attempts to approach the pawn in this way result in stalemate. Bring this situation back a rank and the stalemate problem disappears. Debbie's dithering simply drops the pawn whilst Chuck loses his knight, too (the king can capture it on c6 and still catch the a-pawn). But full marks to Eric.

Points

Amy	1
Bill	1
Chuck	0
Debbie	0
Eric	10

Solution 1-8

Amy's plan would merely improve the scope of Black's bishops and an isolated e-pawn is not an attractive prospect. White has a space advantage and should avoid such trades. Bill's suggestion is silly, anyhow. The main focus of attention should be on the kingside and the f-pawn

112

has a key role to play. Its advance will further cramp Black and there will be chances for a serious attack. White should hold back on ♘d5 until the square is safe. Note that 1 ♘d5 ♘xd5 2 exd5 ♘d4 does not actually lose a pawn.

Points

Amy	0
Bill	0
Chuck	0
Debbie	10
Eric	4

Solution 1-9

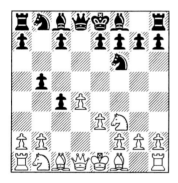

I know it sounds like some sort of fraud but the 'Queen's Gambit' is not really a gambit. Black can take the pawn as in our question but should not really be able to (safely) keep it. If Black is allowed to complete his development the pawn on c4 will be a real thorn throughout the middlegame for, although the c-pawns are doubled, they are still of value. Amy cuts to the chase and her plan, in combination with Deb-

bie's, would work a treat. For example: 1 a4 c6 (the only way to retain the pawn chain) 2 b3 cxb3 3 axb5

White will regain the pawn, achieving the Queen's Gambit's primary aim of setting up a good pawn centre and then using the open lines to pressurise Black's queenside.

Points

Amy	10
Bill	0
Chuck	0
Debbie	2
Eric	0

Solution 1-10

Again the stalemate problem rears its ugly head in Eric's suggestion. Usually in endgames, supported passed pawns are a good thing, but after 1 b7 White will never be able to prevent the black king from oscillating between b8 and c7.

Bill would be taking a risk: after 1 ♗b7 axb6 White has to be sure not to let the b-pawn become a deflection that ultimately wins the a-pawn. Indeed 2 ♗c6, preparing to park on b5, would then be the only way to avoid this as the white king is too far away to catch the b-pawn.

As this was a negative question, the marks below, of course, still refer to how you scored rather than how well our characters performed.

Points

Amy	0
Bill	2
Chuck	0
Debbie	0
Eric	10

Solutions To Test Two

Solution 2-1

It is true that the black king has a strong post in the centre but the key to this ending is the supported passed a4-pawn (sorry, Amy, but White will not be so obliging as to advance it prematurely!). White can play 1 ♔e2 with the intention of aiming for the h-file to hunt Black's two pawns. The black king will be unable to protect them as it must remain within the required zone to track the advance of the a-pawn. Indeed it must stay in the square with corners a4, a8, e8 and e4, and so simple mathematics must be applied should Black wish to capture the b3-pawn with 1...♔c3. It would take Black a further five moves to queen the b-pawn, whereas White, moving first in the race, takes just

four moves to promote. These are the sort of calculations that Eric has made, but his conclusion is wrong. Even if Black waits for the white king to capture on h7 before engaging in this race, he is lost.

Here, for example, White might try 1 ♕e4+ ♔c1 2 ♕c4+ ♔d2 3 ♕b3 ♔c1 4 ♕c3+, forcing the king in front of the pawn. He would then have a tempo to bring back his own king, repeating this pattern until it is sufficiently close to help net the b-pawn.

Points

Amy	0
Bill	0
Chuck	10
Debbie	0
Eric	2

Solution 2-2

Amy's typical beginner's mistake is worth noting. One must be very sure before taking the pressure off the centre in such a manner. It is true that queenside play might come eventually but White has no worries for a long time and can get on with things elsewhere. Bill's ...h7-h6 and ...g7-g5, though inspirational (as ...g5-g4 would pressurise d4 further), unfortunately creates holes and weaknesses, but I am going to award some points to Debbie because the f-pawn often has an important role to play for Black in the French Defence. I just feel here that Black already has some serious pressure on d4 and 1...f6 is a touch greedy and a little premature.

Chuck has the right idea as f5 is a great square for a knight. When the centre is blocked there is not the usual urgency to castle and, consequently, Black shouldn't worry so much about his dark-squared bishop. Although apparently lacking squares, Black's 'good' bishop (i.e. operating on the opposite colour complex to the fixed pawns) is a valuable piece. Eric's option will leave it offside and likely to be forced to trade for White's 'bad' bishop or a knight.

Points

Amy	0
Bill	0
Chuck	10
Debbie	3
Eric	1

Solution 2-3

I've rarely seen so much nonsensical waffle! There are so many analytical flaws this time. Sorry Chuck, that's rubbish, and Eric's 1 ♖c1 bxc1♕+ (actually, even 1...c2+ wins!) 2 ♔xc1 c2 3 ♔b2 ♔d2 is not a draw. I will give something to the elaborate draws (Amy, look out for that 1 ♖b3 b1♕+ 2 ♖xb1 c2+ combination) of Amy and Bill but White should be trying to win. Check out the following position.

The king is just where it wants to be on c2 as the pawns are well controlled. The only pothole for White to avoid is playing ♖xc3, when the king finds itself over-worked after ...b1♕+. However, a 'passing' move such as 1 ♖c7 would force Black's king to move when White can safely capture the c3-pawn on his next turn.

Full marks to Debbie. Finally, Eric, rooks belong *behind* passed pawns (and not passively blockading them).

Points

Amy	1
Bill	1
Chuck	0
Debbie	10
Eric	0

Solution 2-4

There is no entry on the queenside for the white king and that rules out Amy's proposal. Alas 1 h4 h5 and 1 g4 g5 also leave White unable to attack any pawns (note that 2 g4

g6 and 2 h4 h6, respectively, keep the position sealed).

Bill, perhaps, deserves some-thing, but after 1 ♔e3 h5 2 ♔f3 g5 again White will be denied access.

I must confess that this is trick-ier than I first intended, but it does demonstrate how subtlety is occasionally required even in the most ostensibly straightforward positions.

1 ♔e3 is correct, when 1...g5 should be met with 2 h4! when, if Black tries to keep the position closed with 2...g4, it is important that White intercepts Black's in-tended support by putting his own pawn on h5. Similarly after 1...h5, 2 g4! h4 3 g5 is necessary. Black can control the f5-square with 3...g6 but his h-pawn will fall.

Points

Amy	0
Bill	3
Chuck	10
Debbie	0
Eric	0

Solution 2-5

Assuming the previously played h2-h4 was not a red herring, it is a reasonable indicator as to how White should be handling the position. Indeed it would even be a detrimental insertion if White considered a plan featuring f3-f4 and e4-e5, since this would involve completely conceding the g4-square (a nice place for a black knight).

Black has played a Sicilian Dragon and White has selected the sharpest response: the Yugoslav Attack. Both sides should go on the offensive, with Black generally encouraged to attack with pieces rather than pawns. Note that a pawn storm would be too slow for him as White has not moved any pawns around his king, and thus creating open lines for the black rooks would take that much longer. This is why disturbing the a2-pawn would be an undesirable addition to White's set-up. Okay Eric, ♔b1 is a typically useful waiting move but the rest is way too casual. Only

Debbie has got to the point. 1 g4, intending 2 h5, 1 ♗h6 or indeed 1 h5 are all appropriate. Time is of the essence and the first to checkmate wins!

Points

Amy	0
Bill	0
Chuck	1
Debbie	10
Eric	0

Solution 2-6

Amy, Bill and Debbie should all discover how annoying isolated pawns can be in king and pawn endgames as the king is only a short-range piece. Again this puzzle requires the ability to count and think ahead. Chuck has a nice idea but, unfortunately, it is flawed because in his suggested sequence Black has 3...♔b8 to foil White's plan of advancing his king to help promotion. Instead Eric has the tempo theme worked out nicely. After 1 ♔d5 g4 2 ♔d6 g3 we reach the following position:

Only now does White sacrifice his pawn with 3 a8♕+ ♔xa8 4 ♔c7 g2 5 b7+ ♔a7 6 b8♕+ ♔a6 7 ♕b6 mate.

Points

Amy	0
Bill	0
Chuck	2
Debbie	0
Eric	10

Solution 2-7

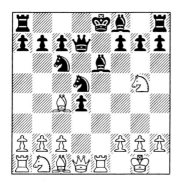

Was 'Cheeky' Chuck trying to pull the wool over our eyes? After 1 ♘xf7, of course, 1...0-0-0 would be

illegal as the knight covers d8. For that matter 1...♗xf7 is also not allowed (ruling out Bill's answer). Certainly 1...♕xf7 is possible but then 2 ♗xd5 is good for White as the e6-bishop is pinned.

That leaves just 1...♔xf7. Here 2 ♕f3+ is remarkably awkward. If the king returns to the e-file then the pin there means that White regains his piece on d5. 2...♔g8 would run into 3 ♖xe6 ♕xe6 4 ♗xd5 and that only really leaves venturing into the open with 2...♔g6. It is important to note how the bishop on c1 controls useful squares even though it hasn't yet moved, and 3 ♖xe6+ ♕xe6 4 ♗d3+ leads to mate. Congratulations Amy!

Points

Amy	10
Bill	0
Chuck	0
Debbie	0
Eric	1

Solution 2-8

Amy has got to grips with the concept of good and bad bishops but her plan is a little optimistic, particularly as it concedes the g5-square to an enemy knight. 1...a4 is easily foiled by 2 b4, which is annoying, since the knight wants to be secure on the excellent c5-post. I cannot see that ♗g5 is exactly a serious threat and Chuck must be sure before playing a move like ...g6-g5 as it makes his dark-squared bishop worse and concedes the f5-square. At least Eric has ambitions, although the ...b7-b5 break is very difficult to arrange now that the a-pawn is on a5.

Who can argue with Debbie? All of her ideas carried some weight and the pawn break ...f7-f5 is standard in the King's Indian Defence.

One useful tip to remember when stuck for a plan is that you should play more on the side of the board that your fixed pawns lean towards. Here, the pawns on d6 and e5 lean towards the kingside.

Points

Amy	2
Bill	0
Chuck	0
Debbie	10
Eric	2

Solution 2-9

It is an important concept to try and advance the pawns first to the opposite-coloured squares to your bishop. For example, after Amy's 1

f6, Black can obtain an easy light-squared blockade with 1...♗d3. Better would be 1 g6+ were it not for the fact that 1...♚f6 wins the f-pawn, while the black bishop keeps a watchful eye over the g8-square.

Advancing the king is often a reasonable idea but here 1 ♚h7 allows 1...♗d3, e.g. 2 g6+ ♚f6 and Black collects the f-pawn and can still cover g8. Consequently Debbie appears to have a point, until we consider Chuck's plan. For example: 1 ♗d4 ♗d3 2 g6+ ♚g8 (on f8 the king will anyway be checked later) 3 ♚g5 ♗c2 4 f6

The threat (which last move would also have forced the same response) is now f6-f7+ with the pawn and bishop combining to guarantee promotion. Hence 4...♗b3 5 ♔f4 ♗c4 6 ♔e5 ♗b3 7 ♔d6 ♔f8 (hindering the simple ♔e7 and f7+) 8 ♔d7 ♗a4+ 9 ♔d8 ♗b3 10 ♗c5+ ♔g8 11 ♔e7 and 12 f7+ is unstoppable. A bit of work but well worth the time invested.

It is useful to note that the following position would be drawn:

If White plays 1 e6+ Black can concede his bishop for both of the pawns. White must keep f5 protected and the black bishop (currently on the best defensive diagonal) should oscillate between c8 and d7.

Points

Amy	0
Bill	2
Chuck	10
Debbie	1
Eric	1

Solution 2-10

It is always worth looking out for checks as there might be a good one! Eric is correct in that respect. Take a look at 1...c6 2 ♗xf7+ ♔e7 3 ♗a3+. Yes, it's goodbye to the black queen! A clever piece of analysis, however, runs 1...♘f6 2 ♗xf7+ ♔xf7 3 ♕xd8 ♗b4+ 4 ♕d2 when the material situation – and the game – is level.

Sadly Debbie didn't go with her 1...♗b4+ idea although she would have needed to keep an eye out for a future ♕a4+. The g7-pawn hanging is also obviously a major feature (sorry, Bill – no points as I suspect you hadn't noticed ♗xf7+ either!).

I'm afraid there is only 1 point for Eric, who had at least noticed the danger to his queen.

Points

Amy	10
Bill	0
Chuck	0
Debbie	0
Eric	1

Solutions To Test Three

Solution 3-1

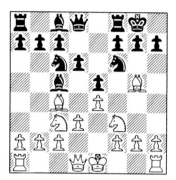

Bill's choice is easily the most aggressive and certainly justified in these circumstances. As the centre is closed there is no great hurry to castle. Chuck's knight on d5 would look good but it can be kicked away later and, as he observes, it is not good to concede the bishop.

It pains me to see juniors frequently advancing their rook's pawns one square to avoid pins although, admittedly, an earlier ...h7-h6 would have prevented the weaknesses that will be incurred after 1 ♘d5. Black's f-pawns will be doubled, thus shattering the defensive pawn structure in front of Black's king. White will have the option of ♘xf6 gxf6 and then posting his

bishop on h6, or ♗xf6 gxf6, when a ♕d2-h6 manoeuvre could be particularly dangerous. The black king might easily suffer as a result of the half-open g-file.

Points

Amy	1
Bill	10
Chuck	1
Debbie	0
Eric	1

Solution 3-2

The beauty of endgames is making the most of what you have left. A well known concept is that a rook's pawn and an opposite-coloured bishop to the queening square fail to beat a lone king camped in the correct corner. The members of our panel observed this but 1 g4 ♘xg4, and 1 h3 ♘h5+, intending ...♘xg3, allow just that simplification.

Debbie is way too optimistic as she won't be able to hunt down Black's knight without the help of pawns to cover key squares. Full marks, though, to Eric. Play this one out for yourself but take care. Don't let the knight remove your g-pawn and be sure to retain at least some control of the dark squares.

Points

Amy	0
Bill	1
Chuck	1
Debbie	0
Eric	10

Solution 3-3

It is good to see that the majority of our characters are beginning to appreciate the concept of making a pawn break (typically, using a pawn to challenge an enemy fixed pawn) to create open or half-open files

for rooks. Eric should note that the half-open b-file is clearly primarily of use to Black, whose rook is not obstructed. Alas, playing 1 d4 is not sensible. Of course the pawn would not remain in the centre after it is taken and White would merely have succeeded in undoubling Black's c-pawns. Moreover the position would then become open and Black is in possession of the bishop pair that would then be granted more scope.

To suggest that Bill's idea is ambitious would be something of an understatement. There are no white rooks on the h-file to benefit from its opening and, furthermore, White has no control over the h5-square. Note that 1 h4 is, in fact, detrimental, as a gaping hole suddenly appears on g4.

On the other hand, Chuck has made a very reasonable suggestion. Giving him a few moves, the position could be as follows:

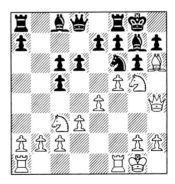

We have been a little harsh on Black here, but White suddenly has a very strong attack. For example he threatens 1 &xg7 &xg7 2 fxg6 with an exchange sacrifice on f6 and the queen's arrival on h7.

Clearly, then, the bishop has options from c1, and the pawn push f4-f5 also brings the rook into play on the f-file. Rook 'swingers' to the third rank and along are certainly not unheard of. Certainly ♖f3-h3 might be a contender (eventually) in our puzzle, but ♖a3-b3 looks bizarre!

Also worth noting is that, in responding to f4-f5, were Black ever to try the greedy ...gxf5, then his king could easily suffer from exposure on the g-file.

Points

Amy	1
Bill	0
Chuck	10
Debbie	1
Eric	0

Solution 3-4

Eric's move is simply poor as it provides White with targets (e.g. the c6-pawn). There is no way that Black can win the white rook because even if it could be attacked White has the very reasonable h3-h4 in order to vacate the h3-square. Amy has a very sensible suggestion but Debbie is mistaken. There is no flaw in the calculation of her recommended sequence but Black is better in this position.

Full marks go to Bill. Before the white king can make it to e2 he has 1...♖fd8 2 ♖d1 ♖d4

By maximizing the use of his rooks in this manner Black will guarantee the win of a pawn. He is taking advantage of the pin on the d-file, with 3...♖xe4 the threat. In response to 3 e5 he can move either rook to d5, when that would be the end of the road for at least one white pawn. Additionally, upon capturing its target a black rook will be left in an excellent position.

Points

Amy	4
Bill	10

Chuck   0
Debbie   0
Eric   0

Solution 3-5

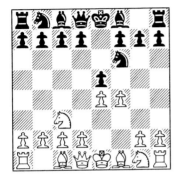

Great judgement from Debbie! Black cannot allow White to build up a broad pawn centre so easily, which is what happens in the majority of the suggested cases, e.g. 1...♘c6 2 fxe5 ♘xe5 3 d4 with a big centre.

It is true that one must be careful about exposing the king along the b6-g1 and, indeed, the h4-e1 diagonals when advancing an f-pawn (and equivalent diagonals when Black). However, Bill's bishop will soon be shut out as White sets up a massive centre.

There is a little bit of sympathy for Amy who, at least, will retain a pawn in the centre. However, the resulting middlegame may eventually turn out as in Question 8 of Test 1. Black's position will be far too passive.

As 1...exf4 2 e5 ♘g8 is not great

Black should focus on 1...d5!. Opening theory would tell you more about this specific position, but just be aware that ...d7-d5 is often a key move for Black in symmetrical e-pawn openings.

Points

Amy	1
Bill	0
Chuck	0
Debbie	10
Eric	0

Solution 3-6

Amy's calculations are completely irrelevant as the black king will protect the h3-pawn and win the h2-pawn. Eric has a very nice idea but after, for example, 1 ♔f5 ♔g2 2 ♔f4 ♔xh2 the white king only reaches f3. As it is not on f2, Black then has 3...♔g1 and the pawn will promote.

Critical, therefore, is the race with, for instance, 1 ♔f5 ♔g2 2 ♔e6 ♔xh2 3 ♔d7 ♔g3 4 ♔xc7 h2 5 ♔b8 (and not 5 ♔b7?, when the c-pawn would find itself pinned by the new black queen) 5...h1♛ 6 c7

Both Chuck and Debbie did their sums right but Debbie has her endgame theory wrong. With rook's pawns and bishop's pawns (i.e. seventh rank pawns on the a-, c-, f- or h-files) there are stalemate tricks that come into play. Here the attacking king is too far away and White need not allow his own king to obstruct the pawn since, when Black's queen ultimately gives check on b6, for example, White can simply place his king on a8 because ...♛xc7 is stalemate. Consequently Black is denied the opportunity to return his king to active duty.

Top marks, then, to Chuck's suggestion.

Points

Amy	0
Bill	0
Chuck	10
Debbie	1
Eric	1

Solution 3-7

Nice principle, Chuck, but that's a ridiculous suggestion here as either pawn will promote immediately. A queen versus rook scenario is very unattractive and, with the defender's rook so far away from the king it is likely to be lost very quickly.

The clever idea is 1 ♖g1!. Black's king cannot advance to c2 due to 2 ♖xg2+ and, even if it made it to a2, the g-pawn can be taken as then the rook pins the b-pawn to the king. White must remain on his toes, though. For example after 1...♚d3 2 ♚b7 ♚e3 Black threatens 3...♚f2, when the only drawing move is 3 ♖b1 with the same scenario as before. Well done Debbie!

Points

Amy	0
Bill	0
Chuck	0
Debbie	10
Eric	0

Solution 3-8

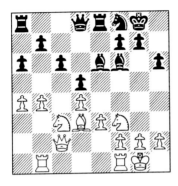

Solution 3-9

Amy is spot on with 1 b5 because this is the correct way to set about creating open or half-open files for White's rooks. If Black wishes to avoid isolated pawns the result will be a backward c6-pawn, presenting White with a juicy target. If Black captures twice on b5 the result will be the afore-mentioned isolated pawns which will also create juicy weaknesses for the white pieces.

Centralisation of rooks is only recommended when there is something for them to do and, unfortunately for Chuck, knights do not benefit from open positions!

Eric has a point, but White needs to crack open the queenside to make genuine progress.

Points

Amy	10
Bill	0
Chuck	0
Debbie	0
Eric	2

Chuck's argument is irrelevant as the black king is nowhere to be seen. Indeed Eric appears to have carried out some bizarre analysis, too. Presumably he was hoping to achieve something like the position below.

There is no way that Black could have arranged this but, even if he did, he is completely lost! It is true that without the bishop White cannot extricate his king and in fact it is stalemate. However, 1 ♗e5+ ♔c8 2 ♗f4 forces the black king to effectively vacate the premises, when

127

3 ♔b7 secures victory.

Thanks for your opinion Debbie, but it's Bill who takes the money. Play it out for yourself and you will discover that with reasonable play from White, the knight will be deprived of squares. Indeed this is a good demonstration of why a short-range knight is usually inferior to a bishop in endgames.

Points

Amy	0
Bill	10
Chuck	0
Debbie	0
Eric	0

Solution 3-10

Phew! This was a difficult one where some serious thinking ahead was required – in which, no doubt, ghosts appeared from time to time. After this and the previous question you should be an expert at this type of endgame by now.

Debbie puts the correct answer forward. Note after 1...♔c7 2 ♘g3 ♔c8 3 ♘f5 ♔c7 4 ♘d6 Black is forced to abandon c8, thus letting the white king out of the corner.

If, on the other hand, the above position was reached with White to play, then he will never be able to control c7 or c8 at the required moment. It's true, honestly! By all means send the knight out on a day trip to the other corners but, when it returns, it will still be no better off!

Thanks to Eric for a clarification of the rules, but what is he talking about?

Points

Amy	0
Bill	0
Chuck	1
Debbie	10
Eric	0

Solutions To Test Four

Solution 4-1

Let us take a look at how play might progress: 1 ♔c3 ♚b6 (after 1...♚a4, White's only way to win is 2 b5! ♔xb5 3 ♚b3) 2 ♔c4 ♚c6 3 b5+ ♚b6 4 ♔b4 ♚b7 5 ♔c5 ♚c7 6 b6+ ♚b7 7 ♔b5 ♚b8 (note that this is vital as 7...♚c8 8 ♔c6 ♚b8 9 b7 ♚a7 10 ♔c7 forces promotion) 7 ♔c6 ♚c8 8 b7+ ♚b8. Without the b2-pawn the game should end in stalemate but its presence, providing an effective 'passing' move, means that Black is forced to give way. After 9...♚a7 10 ♔c7 the game is over. It was not necessary to have something to control the promotion square, only something that would transfer the move to Black.

Below is a different matter:

White can play 1 d4 here because he then has the 'opposition'. The two kings are opposed but it is BLACK to move and he must give way. After, for example, 1...♚e7 2 ♔c6 ♚d8 3 ♚d6 White has the opposition. It is worth remembering that, whoever is to move in such a situation, if the attacker gets his king on the sixth rank in front of the pawn, then he will win. After 3...♚c8 4 ♚e7 ♚c7 5 d5 the pawn is ushered through.

Debbie is confused. The only file on which none of this is successful is a rook's file.

Points

Amy	1
Bill	0

Chuck 10
Debbie 0
Eric 0

Solution 4-2

None of the suggested moves is poor, although Debbie's comes close to unintentionally providing Black's rooks with some action, e.g. 1 a4 b5 2 a5 b4 etc. Chuck has a point. Normally centralising rooks means placing them on the two centre files but you can't get more central than d4!

The maximum score, though, is for Eric, who gets to the most critical plan the quickest. The problem with 1 ♔g2 is that Black is given his big opportunity to challenge the vital open file with 1...♖d8 (with White having no time to double and thus dominate).

Points

Amy 1
Bill 0
Chuck 5
Debbie 0
Eric 10

Solution 4-3

I thought I'd better feature one of my own games, so:

**Merriman-Ward
Isle of Man 1994**
1 d4 ♘f6 2 c4 e6 3 ♘c3 ♗b4 4 e3 b6 5 ♘ge2 ♘e4 6 f3 ♘xc3 7 ♘xc3 ♗xc3+ 8 bxc3 ♘c6 9 ♗d3 ♕h4+ 10 g3 ♕h3 11 ♕e2 ♗a6 12 ♗a3 0-0-0 13 f4 d5 14 0-0-0 ♘a5 15 c5 ♗xd3 16 ♖xd3 ♘c4

Black has a fantastic outpost for the knight, providing a stark contrast with White's bad bishop.
17 ♗b2 ♕f5 18 ♖f1 h5 19 ♖e1

130

**♕e4 20 ♕c2 ♔b7 21 a4 f5 22 h4
♖h6 23 ♕e2 ♖g6 24 ♖g1 ♔c6 25
cxb6 axb6 26 ♔c2 ♖a8 27 ♔b3
♖xa4 28 ♔xa4 ♕xd3 0-1**

Quite instructive (if I say so myself!) and from this you can deduce that I will give Debbie the maximum score. I manoeuvred my queen to h3 deliberately so that it would prove an inconvenience, being very unlikely to be trapped unless I incarcerated it, for example, with my own h-pawn! Castling queenside entailed no serious risks.

Points

Amy	0
Bill	0
Chuck	0
Debbie	10
Eric	2

Solution 4-4

The only accurate answer, in fact, comes from Bill. The first part *only* of both Chuck and Debbie's statements ring true, and Eric's proposed sequence leads to a draw.

The point is that here 1...♔h1 leaves Black with no moves, so 2 ♔c6 would be stalemate. But with a black pawn on, for example, a4(!), then 2 ♕f2 forces mate next move. A queen will defeat any pawn only on the sixth rank. Have a bit of fun by trying a few permutations out for yourself.

Points

Amy	0
Bill	10
Chuck	1
Debbie	1
Eric	0

Solution 4-5

These sort of questions should be food and drink to you by now!

Bill is completely mistaken. Although mathematically a ♗+♘ = ♖+♙ = 6 points, in reality a knight and bishop are much more useful (certainly in the opening/middlegame) than a rook which, traditionally, tends to see less action until the endgame. Chuck seeks to change that, and going for the pawn break that will create a half-open file for at least one rook (possibly to be used later by the other rook) is the most attractive plan.

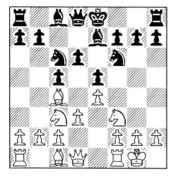

Surely White would not have placed his bishop on c4 only to relocate it to b5 so soon. Doubled pawns are not always bad news and a pawn on c6 would control what is otherwise a handy outpost on d5. In fact a white knight would love a permanent home on d5. However, that will not happen after 1 ᐃd5, but a 1 ♗g5(xf6) plan has its merits, although the problem with effectively 'pinning' a knight to a bad bishop is that if the knight moves you are offered an unappealing trade.

While I am frequently critical of little unnecessary pawn moves on the flanks, I accept that 1 h3 fulfils a purpose. Moves such as ♗d2 and ♖e1, however, appear only to be moving pieces for the sake of moving them. In my book (yes, this one!) they certainly do not constitute

developing moves.

Points

Amy	0
Bill	0
Chuck	10
Debbie	1
Eric	4

Solution 4-6

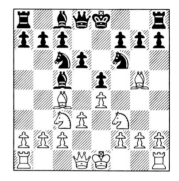

Okay – I will finally give something for 1...♗b4 and the concept of moving one piece twice before moving others once (usually avoided).

The centre is blocked and so the kings are safe where they stand for the moment. Sorry, Amy but this book has already seen how annoying a shattered kingside pawn structure can be around the castled king, and that will be the outcome after 1...0-0 2 ᐃd5. I really like Bill's aggressive riposte that questions the ambition of White's entire approach.

Debbie's interesting answer doesn't actually avoid the doubled pawns. After 1...ᐃe7 2 ♗xf6 gxf6

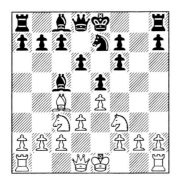

the queen prevents 4 ♖h1+ and Black should go on to win.

they might not be such a problem because Black has not castled, but they are still not ideal.

Eric's solution reminds me of five-year-old juniors who merely copy each other's moves. You may come across a few king and pawn endings where you would rather not have to move but in the majority of cases it is better to, and having the advantage of the move can often be decisive.

Points

Amy	0
Bill	10
Chuck	3
Debbie	2
Eric	0

Solution 4-7

It is always nice to hear Eric contribute, but a draw is a draw however you achieve it!

I would love to award Bill points for pure 'sneakiness' but, alas, the flaw in his analysis comes with 2 ♔a3 a1♕+ 3 ♔b3 ♕a8!. Oops! Yes,

I think that Debbie was wrong about Chuck, who had everything under control. His whole idea is 1 ♖h2+ ♔b1 2 ♔b3. As mate is threatened on the back rank, the only move is 2...a1♘+, but after 3 ♔c3 one can see why knights are pretty pathetic in corners.

Either the knight is lost straight away or 3...♔c1 4 ♖h1 is mate.

Points

Amy	0
Bill	0

Chuck	10
Debbie	0
Eric	0

Solution 4-8

Take a look at Chuck's move 1 ♖a5:

Cutting off the enemy king is an important theme in endgames as the king is a very useful piece when not worried about being mated. Obviously the point is that the black king cannot advance, and after 1...h3 2 ♖a3 the monarch is of no help to its pawn, e.g. 2...h2 3 ♖h3. Yes, we have not seen so much evidence of it thus far in this book but rooks

really do enjoy being behind passed pawns. The rook stops the pawn from successfully promoting and, of course, simply threatens to take it. And notice that White's king can approach the pawn at leisure. Of course if the king traverses the fifth rank in front of the rook then the invisible barrier will be (temporarily) broken. However, if White is really sadistic he can nudge his rook to the side and cross the rank on the far side, thus highlighting the frustration of Black's king.

Points

Amy	1
Bill	1
Chuck	10
Debbie	1
Eric	1

Solution 4-9

I will award a point to Amy for being happy to develop and to Chuck for his novel idea (I don't actually like it very much, though, as Black's king could be a target on the h-file after h4-h5, for example).

However, Debbie is the only character who gets to the crux of the matter. After 1...c5 Black frees the queen and can set about mounting pressure on the d4-pawn. White can't take on c5 without destroying his pawn structure, and Black would regain the pawn anyway.

Bill has got a bit confused (it is rash wing play that should be met by action in the centre!) and I am afraid Eric's ramblings are simply too passive for my liking!

Points

Amy	1
Bill	0
Chuck	1
Debbie	10
Eric	0

Solution 4-10

Chuck's idea has no place here as the black king is already up with the action and 1 ♖h3 allows the g-pawn to advance with tempo. Debbie's answer is lacking in informa-

tion and cannot be rewarded. The fact is that White will not win unless the king assists the rook in halting the g-pawn. As it happens, Eric's line would work if he replaced 3 ♖a4 *and* was granted a big gift.

In the diagram position, after 3 ♔d2 g2 4 ♖g7 ♔f3 5 ♔e1, for example, Black would be in zugzwang (i.e. not wanting to move for fear of losing his g-pawn) *If*, that is, he didn't have a b-pawn. But he does, so this is merely a fantasy variation designed to point out that the attacking king needs to be in touch with the g-pawn sooner.

Full marks go to Amy. Connected passed pawns can be dangerous but here Black's are not yet sufficiently advanced to pose enough danger to the awesome white rook.

Points

Amy	10
Bill	0
Chuck	1
Debbie	1
Eric	0

Solutions To Test Five

Solution 5-1

Debbie has a pretty reasonable way to achieve a draw but, even if it does not ultimately win, Eric's plan is clearly the most ambitious.

1 a4 a6 2 ♖a3 – note that 2 ♖a2 would have the same effect – reaches the position below:

Now, of course Black, cannot double with 2...♖a7 as the pawn is pinned after 3 axb5. Therefore Black might play 2...♖e8, for example, but the e-file holds little promise. In contrast 3 ♖ba1 forces the a8-rook to abandon its post, leaving White free to trade pawns and infiltrate with his rooks. If at any time Black plays ...bxa4, then his isolated a-pawn will be a liability.

Chuck's idea would have the reverse effect of gifting Black the a-file on which to attack pawns, while who knows what is going on in Bill's mind? The a- and e- files are the only realistic options for the rooks.

Points

Amy	1
Bill	0
Chuck	0
Debbie	1
Eric	10

Solution 5-2

Could it really be that our panel's answers are getting more and more plausible? Well, not in Bill's case this time. A pawn on c6 would be a solid defender (in queen's pawn openings the b8-knight often develops on d7 anyway) so White would simply be giving Black a free move.

Regarding Debbie's answer, there is something to be said for moving pieces to squares that you know you are going to use before ones about which you are not sure. However, in order to generate any serious activity on the queenside White will have to engage in a 'minority attack' (the likes of which we have already seen). The rook on c1 will do little unless the inevitable 'rock' pawn on c6 is negotiated. The plan b2-b4-b5 traditionally addresses this point, so the rook may be required on b1 (the other rook can come to c1 later, if appropriate).

The f5-bishop is an inconvenience to White and one can understand Eric's solution. However, the fact is that Black should be punished for abandoning the b7-pawn so early. Chuck's plan may appear to bring the queen out a little prematurely, but there is no denying that it will win a whole pawn for precious little material. Although games with combinations, tactics and sacrificial

mating attacks may stick in our minds more often, the truth is that the majority of games are won by gaining a material lead, exchanging pieces and converting the endgame. Yes, once more I'm going to say it: a pawn is a pawn!

Points

Amy	1
Bill	0
Chuck	10
Debbie	1
Eric	2

Solution 5-3

After 1 ♔c5 ♔c7 – or, indeed, 1 ♔e5 ♔e7 – White can make no progress as the black king matches its opposite number and prevents an infiltration. Instead it is White who can gain the 'opposition' with 1 ♔d5! I suppose 1...♔c7 puts up the best fight but then 2 ♔c5 renews the opposition once more. This time, when Black gives way with 2...♔b7, White can jump in with 3 ♔d6. The fact is that, although it is near them at the moment, the black king will soon be forced away from defending the pawns, e.g. 3...♔a8 4 ♔c6 ♔a7 5 ♔c7 ♔a8 6 ♔b6.

Chuck's interesting theory would arise, for example, after 2...♔d7 3 ♔b6 ♔d6 4 ♔xa6 ♔c6

Were we to advance the whole position one rank up the board, then he would have a valid argument. Unfortunately after 1 ♔a7 ♔c7 2 a6 Black must allow either 2...♔c6 3 ♔b8 or 2...♔c8 3 ♔b6.

Points

Amy	0
Bill	10
Chuck	2
Debbie	0
Eric	0

Solution 5-4

There are some reasonable arguments put forward by all of the members of our panel and I would also have been pleased to hear 1 c4 – or even 1 f4 – recommended, which really stakes a claim for central domination.

Generally the argument is that knights 'know' where they want to go whereas bishops have more options, prompting us to see what the opponent does before being committed – hence the 'knights before bishops' general opening rule and my favouring the answers given by Debbie and Amy. As it seems most likely that White will castle kingside it is logical that White should therefore give preference to developing the pieces on that side of the board. On c3 a pin of the knight by ...♗b4 – though far from the end of the world – may be encouraged, and the e-pawn can be defended by ♗d3 which, when the e-pawn inevitably advances, will present White with a promising diagonal.

Points

Amy	7
Bill	0
Chuck	0
Debbie	10
Eric	1

Solution 5-5

This is a study-like position and Chuck deserves the top mark. Play might continue as follows: 1 ♔e8 ♚e6 2 ♔d8 ♚d6 3 ♔c8 ♚c6 4 ♔b8 ♚b6 5 ♔a8 ♚c6 6 ♔a7 ♚c7 7 ♔a6 ♚c6 8 ♔a5 ♚c5 9 ♔a4 ♚c4

Now after 10 ♔a3 Black cannot play 10...♚c3 as the king would then be out of the 'square' of the white f-pawn. Consequently we might see something like 10...♚d4 11 ♔b4 ♚e4 12 ♔c4 ♚f5 13 ♔d5 ♚f6 14 ♔e4 ♚e6 15 f5+ ♚f6 16 ♔f4, when White would win the g-pawn and the game.

I must admit that this was difficult, but it is nonetheless very informative. Eric is wrong about all except Bill's answer. White will queen his pawn and then Black will push his to the seventh rank. As it is a knight's pawn you should know by now that with a little work White will win.

Points

Amy	0
Bill	0
Chuck	10
Debbie	2
Eric	0

Solution 5-6

Only computers are able to analyse all of the checks involved if the defender's rook wanted to safely leave its king. In practice most humans would end up losing their rook, e.g. 1 ♖b8 ♕f1+ 2 ♔d2 ♕g2+ 3 ♔d1 (or 3 ♔f3 ♕g3+) 3...♕h1+ 4 ♔e2 ♕h2+.

Although 1 ♖b3+?? does give

away the rook for nothing (1...♕xb3!) in fact White does have a stalemate theme to help him salvage a draw. With 1 ♖a2+ the rook can't be captured on a2, nor indeed on a3 after 1...♔b3 2 ♖a3+. Hence 1...♔b4, but after 2 ♖b2+ there will be no shelter for the king on the a- or b-files, while 2...♔c3 runs into 3 ♖b3+. There are no stalemates with the king on c4 but after 2...♔c4 3 ♖c2+ the rook cannot cross the d-file either due to 4 ♖d2.

The vast majority of times the queen should win and the key is not bringing the queen too close, thus avoiding stalemate tricks.

Here, with White to play, the queen has kept its distance. The king is turning the screw and there are no stalemate ideas. The rook is forced to abandon its king but wherever it goes it will quickly be lost through a sequence of checks, e.g. 1 ♖b8 ♕e4+ 2 ♔a1 ♕h1+ 3 ♔a2 (note that 3 ♖b1 temporarily saves the rook but 3...♕a8 is mate) 3...♕h2+.

Points

Amy	0
Bill	10
Chuck	0
Debbie	1
Eric	0

Solution 5-7

Incorporated in a number of our panel's answers are many themes that have already been covered in this book. The drawback in Chuck's answer is that 1 ♔e5 should be met with 1...♔e3. Black should abandon any hope of saving the h6-pawn and instead concentrate on getting back to defend. He would be successful in this task after 2 ♔f5 ♔d4 3 ♔g6 ♔e5 4 ♔xh6 ♔f6 5 ♔h7 ♔f7, when White's king can escape after 6 h6 ♔f8 7 ♔g6 but 7...♔g8 is a draw.

However, this shielding off technique is best employed with 1 ♔e4. White's king can make it to Black's pawn in the same amount of time as with 1 ♔e5 or 1 ♔e6, but this way he deprives Black of vital retreat squares.

Points

Amy	0
Bill	1
Chuck	2
Debbie	0
Eric	10

Solution 5-8

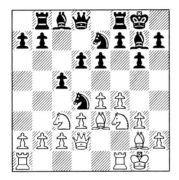

Okay, this was a radical shift in question type. Anyway, Bill is clearly getting to grips with the pawn break concept, and forcing a pawn safely through to f6 would certainly be an achievement. Unfortunately, not only does this hand over the e5-square to Black but most of the enemy pieces have been posted to hinder this advance. Yes, apart from the pawns on e6 and g6, both knights and the c8-bishop have f5 in their sights. Clearly 1 ♘xd4 allows a simple fork, while slightly more difficult to explain is why 1 ♗xd4 is a mistake. Check out the position after the sequence 1...cxd4 2 ♘e2

(see following diagram)

Although Eric's argument may have sounded convincing, there are several drawbacks. He has given Black the advantage of the bishop pair. With ...e6-e5 likely to appear soon, he has left himself with a bad bishop and may suffer in the long-term on the dark squares. He has no chance of winning the d4-pawn and his c2-pawn will also receive some unwanted attention on the now half-open c-file. Although it slightly obstructs the fianchettoed bishop, the d4-pawn is powerfully placed in the centre and will remain a hindrance to White.

Overall, aiming for the advance c2-c3 is the brightest of our panel's suggestions but, alas, Debbie's 1 ♘e2 drops the b2-pawn to the bishop after the d4-knight trades on e2 or f3.

Points

Amy	0
Bill	0
Chuck	10
Debbie	0
Eric	0

The problem with 1 ♖h1 and 1 ♖f1 (there is no significant difference between these moves) is that the black king can escape its current cage with 1...♔c8. Indeed at the moment the defending king is trapped in one of only two corners that it needs to be in in order for White to be victorious. The other is the h1 corner and you will observe that the key factor is the fact that it matches the colour of the bishop. I will return to that point in a moment but first let me highlight that 1 ♖c2 ♗b3 2 ♖b2 is a neat manoeuvre. The bishop cannot retreat to a4 or c4 because the white king would win with a discovered check. This leaves something like 2...♗e6 3 ♖e2 ♗f7 (or 3...♗d7 4 ♖f2, which will transpose) 4 ♖f2 ♗e6 5 ♖f8+ ♗c8, when a rook 'pass' along the eighth rank will lead to mate next move. Note that this would not be the case were it were a dark-squared corner we were talking about:

If White passes in the above position it will be stalemate. By all means try for yourself; you will discover that Black has set up camp in a good corner to defend and, without a blunder, will be able to draw.

So I'm afraid that Debbie is mistaken about her general assessment, although White would still be winning after 1 ♖c7. There is no way out for the black king and White can entertain Eric's plan next time around.

Points

Amy	0
Bill	0
Chuck	2
Debbie	0
Eric	10

Solution 5-10

One should not be too despondent about any initial findings. Sure, 1 ♔f7 ♔h8 2 g6 is, unfortunately, stalemate, and 1 g6+ ♔h8! is annoying, but you should 'know' that

White is winning because his king is well positioned.

Eric is wrong since 1 ♔f5 ♚g7 2 g6 ♚g8! 3 ♔f6 ♚f8, obtaining the opposition, is drawn, but Debbie is right to go with her instincts. Indeed 1 ♔f7 ♚h8 2 ♔g6 is the correct sequence. I said earlier that if a king makes it ahead of its pawn (provided this is not on a rook's file) on the sixth rank the game is won, and here 2...♚g8 3 ♔h6 ♚h8 4 g6 ♚g8 5 g7 ♔f7 6 ♚h7 validates my declaration!

Points

Amy	0
Bill	0
Chuck	1
Debbie	10
Eric	0

Marking Scheme and Scorechart

	Test 1	Test 2	Test 3	Test 4	Test 5
1	10		10	10	
2	1		10	10	
3	2	10	1	2	
4	10	10	0	1	
5	5	10	10	4	
6	10	10	1	3	
7	1	1	10	0	
8	2	10	10	1	
9	2	10	0	10	
10	2	1	10		
Total	43	63	62		

0-20 Er, I can't lie to you – your score isn't too impressive. Try redoing the questions. If your total improves, then at least you have learnt something.

21-40 Not a disaster, but there is clearly plenty of room for improvement. Don't give up, though, as I'm sure you'll get there in the end.

41-60 A very satisfactory score, and you have good reason to be encouraged by your performance.

61-80 You are definitely progressing. A good performance that bodes well for the future!

81-100 An excellent score. Provided you didn't cheat you have good cause to act like the cat who got the cream. There is still much to learn, of course, but you have clearly acquired some valuable knowledge already.